Ms. Faux Pas

DESIGNED BY CARLO BARILE

Ms. Faux Pas

A *Not* *Guide to Glitterati Manners*

BY JOAN KRON

ILLUSTRATIONS BY
MICHAEL WITTE

PARVENU PRESS · NEW YORK

Designed by Carlo Barile
Copyright © 1988 by Joan Kron
All rights reserved.
These essays were previously published serially in
AVENUE magazine in 1986, 1987, 1988.
The characters and situations in this book are fictitious.
Certain established places are mentioned, but the names,
characters, and situations are either the product of the author's
imagination or used fictitiously.
Published by Parvenu Press, Box 73, 205 East 63 Street,
New York, New York 10021
Manufactured in the United States
Library of Congress Catalog Card Number: 88-90783
Kron, Joan.
Ms. Faux Pas: A Non Guide to Glitterati Manners.
Includes index.
1. Essays. 2. Humor. 3. Social Commentary. 4. Manners
I. Witte, Michael, Illustrator. II. Title
ISBN: 0-9620612-0-4
10 9 8 7 6 5 4 3 2 1
First Edition

To Judy and Peter Price,
who never asked the author to take
the bite out of Ms. Faux Pas

and to Lucy Kroll, who
believed it was a book
from the start

Contents

I

Manners

The Back-Talk Show

Back off, *mes amis*. Ms. Faux Pas has just returned from her karate class and she's feeling mean and lean. Don't ask her to say *fromage*. Smiling at people politely but insincerely is definitely passé.

An awareness that the Have-a-Nice-Day era of etiquette was coming to a close hit Ms. Faux Pas like a ton of bricks when she saw George Bushwhacker, the presidential unhopeful, kick anchorperson Dan Rathernot's ash can on the evening news. Suddenly it was apparent that television had entered a new gloves-off phase and that stations would soon have a lot of openings for fiercely attractive guests and hosts with the reflexes of pit bulls—folks who wouldn't hesitate to kick ash cans. Ms. Faux

Pas vowed to be ready should opportunity knock.

Actually, looking back now, Ms. Faux Pas realizes there were many earlier indications that Happy Talk was being knocked out of the ring by Back Talk. Over the last year, at least, there has been a definite decline in the exquisite self-control it takes to keep smiling no matter how badly one is provoked, a quality that used to be considered a sure sign of class.

Suddenly, it seems, the best people are flying off the handle—with no social consequences. What happened after hotheaded Dan Rather-not (in an earlier cause célèbre) lost his cool when his boss, Larry Trisch, allowed a tennis match onto Dan's court, causing Dan to blow a fuse, which left the network in the dark for seven minutes? Did Dan lose his job? *Pas du tout*. After a lot of pros and cons on op-ed pages, Dan's ratings went up, and the consensus was that it's better for an anchorperson to get mad than to cry.

Getting mad is also all the rage in high society, in which there are so many open feuds that no one wants to serve on a seating-arrangement committee any more. It's a terrible job—to fill a table you can hardly find ten people who aren't at each other's throats. And Denny Whodunit, the society tattletale who blitzed his glitterati pals in his latest roman à clef, risks more than a cold shoulder when he ventures out these days. His book, *People Unlike Us*, has alienated so many socialites that a bodyguard has to be hired to sit with him at Mort Mortenson's, society's favorite greasy spoon.

The whole United States Senate couldn't protect George Bushwhacker recently from the wrath of Bob Dole-it-out. If real estate mogul Donald Trumpet, who'll go anywhere for a good fight (and who enjoys picking one if he can't find any), had had advance notice of this Capitol Hill contretemps, he would have bought up all the ringside seats and flown in his hundred best friends.

But perhaps Perry Zipking, First Lady Nancy Reaganomics's favorite social walker, has done the most to make anger socially acceptable. Perry is well known for losing his temper in the most inconvenient places. It's said that he can't have a conversation with a waiter or a taxi driver without kicking ashtrays. Once upon a time, that sort of behavior toward the working class would have been cause for social ostracism, but not now. Today, tough guys finish first. Mr. Zipking is still on the First Lady's A list, although, *entre nous*, at state dinners he is never seated within fifty feet of the head of the taxi drivers' union.

Little wonder that getting mad has done more for interview-show ratings than Dr. Ruth. Back-talk-show host with the most, Morton Downer, spends his whole broadcast trying to rile up his guests and his audience. Child psychologists have theorized that Mr. Downer, a society brat, is revolting against his peer group's method of dealing with animosity: smiling to people's faces and talking behind their backs—preferably to syndicated gossips.

Wifty LeCzar, Ms. Faux Pas's feisty agent, was confident that in this no-holds-barred climate the outspoken Ms. Faux Pas could be a contender. And owing to an amazing stroke of luck, she got her big break before her designer ash can–kicking boots had even been delivered.

There was Ms. Faux Pas, standing in line for the Morton Downer show, at which she was hoping to get some tips on the fine points of dirty debating, when the irascible Mr. Downer stalked out of the studio, fuming that the makeup man had given him Gephardt eyebrows instead of Dukakis eyebrows. Slamming the door behind him, Mr. Downer bellowed that he was going outside to kick ash cans and he didn't care if the channel had to go dark for the rest of the evening while he chilled out.

When Ms. Faux Pas heard the show was about to go black, she was more than disappointed—she was furious. She started kicking ash cans. "I'm mad as hell and I'm not going to take it anymore," she shouted at a studio usher—and faster than you can say *George Bushwhacker*, one of the show's producers collared Ms. Faux Pas and marched her off to makeup. She could hardly believe her luck. She was about to become the host of the *Back-Talk Show*.

When the makeup artist tried to give her a beauty mark like Mr. Downer's, she gave him a karate chop—but she didn't walk out for even one minute.

The guests that night were more than Ms. Faux Pas could have hoped for: George Bushwhacker and Dan Rathernot, together for a return bout. What a way for Ms. Faux Pas to start a new career! The only problem was that Dan and George were now conciliatory. Ms. Faux Pas couldn't get either one to bad-mouth the other. The audience was screaming for blood while George was apologizing for denting Dan's ash can and Dan was asking if George's jugular vein had healed yet.

During the commercial break, the producer whispered to Ms. Faux Pas that Mr. Nielsen had called to report that all over America sets were being turned off—a whole nation was being put to sleep by Dan and George. "Do something!" he screamed. Quickly Ms. Faux Pas huddled with the two guests, warning them that *their* Q ratings—TV's litmus test for personalities' personality—were sinking fast, along with hers.

"Whose idea was it to come out here looking like peacemakers?" she asked them mischieviously. When George insisted that he was at the meeting and didn't know what was being discussed but agreed to go along with it, Dan turned furious. "If you didn't know about it, how could you go along with it?" he screamed. Before you could kick an ash can, the two guests were tearing into each other. Thanks to Ms. Faux Pas, America was awake again.

Well, *vive la confrontation!*

The next time she sees you, Ms. Faux Pas will tell you what she wrote on Morton Downer's cast after he broke his big toe kicking ash cans.

Guess Who's Not
Coming to Dinner?

ttendez une minute while Ms. Faux Pas rushes out to mail a letter. She just received an invitation to a very unusual party, and she's afraid if she waits too long to RSVP, she'll be disinvited.

Disinviting is all the rage on the party circuit—ever since Teeny Mahogany, editor of *Vanity Unfair*, was disinvited to Sally Quince's party after Teeny gave Sally's novel a rotten review. Sally didn't waste a minute wondering how to handle the touchy situation. She took an ad in *Publisher's Weakly* telling Teeny not to bother showing up.

But not all disinviting is done in anger. Ms. Faux Pas's friend Judy Gadabout, for example, disinvites only her dearest friends. Judy can't bear to be alone for even one evening, so she is constantly calling her friends and telling them to save this date or that for a dinner party she is planning—but alas, the invitation is never in the mail. The day before the date being reserved by her designated guests, Judy calls them all and says, "Never mind." Pleading tired blood, a kitchen flood, or a misplaced guest of honor, she disinvites everyone—without even giving them a rain check. Judy will often be spotted on the night of the canceled event—disguised in a red wig—on the town with more scintillating company than she was able to corral for her party.

Ms. Faux Pas has discovered you can also be disinvited by association.

Once upon a time, invitations were invariably for two—and it was a guest's inalienable right to bring a date, a mate, a friend, or a significant other to a party. But today, hostesses are fussier about who accompanies one to dinner than one's mother. And the HRA, the Host's Rights Association, recently decreed that not desiring the company of a guest's escort is grounds for disinviting. Illustrious party-giver Elsa Maison, the hostess with the mostest condos to sell, is ruthless about unauthorized others, especially when the unauthorized are single women. With single men at a premium, she does not want her extra men showing up willy-nilly with uninvited ladies on their arms to mess up her seating arrangements.

Even extra men can be problems. Telling a hostess your escort will be Horst von Polo, the man accused of boring his wife to death, is bound to cause disinvitation in certain circles, and when invited to a dinner party *chez* Dan Rathernot, your invitation will be revoked if you should even suggest bringing your buddy Larry Trisch, Dan's boss.

Disinviting is rampant during the summer at the watering holes of the glitterati, when every homeowner has houseguests. Hostesses used to say politely, "No problem," when a guest asked to bring six of her own guests to the party—but now guests of guests have to apply for dinner party visas, and more often than not, the guest is disinvited because of her guests on the grounds that there are only so many seats at the table. In fact, the problem is so pervasive that invitations now read: "This invitation admits one and is nontransferable."

But even if you plan to come alone you can be persona non grata.

Back when people operated on the principle that "You made your bed, you'll have to lie in it," an invitation was as good as a signed contract. When you were asked to dinner, you could count on not having to cook that night, no matter what books you liked, what company you kept, what company you took over, or what crime you perpetrated between the moment the invitation went out and the day of the party. But today, when people are neither making nor lying in their own beds, one's invitation can be summarily revoked.

Just last week, Ms. Faux Pas was disinvited to what may have been a very interesting luncheon, given by a gentleman she had never met but may have read about in gossip columns. (Ms. Faux Pas has noticed that receiving invitations from strangers is the only thing more prevalent these days then disinviting.) Ms. Faux Pas suspects she was disinvited because she waited too long to RSVP. *Entre nous*, she procrastinated because she couldn't recall who the host was or when she had met him. (Ms. Faux Pas still believes that you don't go to a strange man's apartment, no matter how beautifully engraved the invitation.) But when a genteel secretary followed up the invitation to Mr. DeBold's luncheon with a phone call, wondering if Ms. Faux Pas was planning to attend, she changed her policy—which proved to be a big mistake.

Ms. Faux Pas confided to the secretary that she could not recall being introduced to the gentleman.

But, of course, replied the secretary. Mr. DeBold specializes in giving luncheons for interesting people he'd like to meet. "You've probably read about his parties in Liz ["Blow Up a Story"] Smithereens's column," she said.

Of course.

Ms. Faux Pas admits falling for this sales pitch, possibly aimed at her nouveau insecurity. Ms. Faux Pas's psychic recently divined that Ms. Faux Pas was a glitterata—or would soon become one—and an invitation to Mr. DeBold's seemed to confirm her new glit status.

Well, if you put it *that* way, said Ms. Faux Pas to the amanuensis (the glitterati word for private secretary), "Ms. Faux Pas accepts with pleasure Mr. DeBold's kind invitation."

Luckily, Ms. Faux Pas did not invest in a new frock. The day before the lunch, the amanuensis called again. "There's a terrible problem," she said. "Mr. DeBold's lunch is oversubscribed. So many people said yes that there is no room at the table for them all. Since Ms. Faux Pas is such a dear and close friend of Mr. DeBold's, she is the only one who can be disinvited."

Disinvited? The dreaded word! Deleted from the guest list; zapped from the computer screen. Out in the cold.

"No problem," fibbed Ms. Faux Pas through clenched teeth. She is still black and blue from kicking herself for being polite.

Ms. Faux Pas is counting the ways she is wounded. First, at being disinvited. Second, at being wrongly considered one of Mr. DeBold's best friends. And third, at being disinvited because she is supposed to be one of Mr. DeBold's oldest friends. Is this the way glitterati treat their oldest friends? Any friend who has stuck by Mr. DeBold after repeatedly being invited to make chitchat with total strangers at these weekly luncheons deserves better. But then, what can you expect from a man who can't even remember who his best friends are?

The *Journal of Wall Street Ups and Downs* blames the current "rampant rudeness" on social life becoming too "anonymous." Ms. Faux Pas agrees. The host doesn't know the guest, and—who knows?— the host's secretary may even be a temp who doesn't know her boss. Ms. Faux Pas believes that unless the disinvited take countermeasures, the practice will snowball. She suggests a contradisinvitation campaign. It requires beating the hosts to the calligrapher and sending them a nice note insisting that they don't even think of inviting you to their parties. Ms. Faux Pas's contra card would read:

Dear Mr. DeBold,

Your secretary mentioned to Ms. Faux Pas's hairdresser that Ms. Faux Pas was being invited to your upcoming luncheon. Before you waste a stamp, Ms. Faux Pas wants you to know that her houseguests that week will be Horst von Polo, Larry Trisch, and Teeny Mahogany— and Ms. Faux Pas is planning to take them everywhere she goes. They have all heard about your parties and have specially asked not to be taken to one. Since you are such a good friend, Ms. Faux Pas thought she would tell you the truth rather than fib and tell you she'd be going down the Nile with Ann Go-Getter. Don't bother to give Ms. Faux Pas a rain check. Regards to your charming Telly Girl.

Au revoir,
Ms. Faux Pas

The next time she sees you, Ms. Faux Pas will tell you what happened when she asked Elsa Maison if Ms. Faux Pas's houseguest, Eliza Doolittle, a speech therapy exchange student from London, could accompany Ms. Faux Pas to Elsa's next party.

The Gourmet TV Dinner

*P*ardonnez-moi while Ms. Faux Pas *ouvre*s the *porte* and comes out of the closet where she keeps her TV. For more years than she can remember, Ms. Faux Pas has had to have Wagner playing on the foyer Victrola on Friday nights to drown out the sound of J.R. and Sue Ellen's bickering. As you know, ever since the dawn-ing of the *Flintstones* it has been de rigueur in high society to claim one never watches the tube. But now, with rumors flying that Oliver North-by-northwest will become a TV spokesman for traveler's checks ("Don't Leave for Managua Without Them"), it appears that TV is becoming acceptable.

But few people—or things—make it up the

social ladder these days without a gentle push from public relations.

To win social acceptability, the TV industry had to hire its own PR flack, Howard Reubensandwich, whose strategy was to get important people to watch TV during top social occasions—and admit to it.

The only nights on which watching TV while having a civil conversation is condoned and accepted in public are Election Night and Academy Awards Night. On all other nights, TV has been a private indulgence for the glitterati—and a guilt-ridden one. Let's face it, if they're not ashamed of it, why do they all hide their sets inside expensive built-ins?

But today at last, thanks to Howard Reubensandwich, TV is emerging from behind the cabinetmakers' hand-polished mahogany doors.

The hottest social divertissement is the TV dinner, and hostesses are rushing down to Crazy Freddy's, the TV dinner party rental store, to rent their TV monitors, microphones, and recliners and to get blowups of old *TV Guide* covers to decorate their bashes.

The TV dinner craze was launched with chic little fundraising dos at the Museum of Networking, Bill Paleface's new pet project. Something had to be done to save *The Flying Nun* from being carted off to the slumber room in the video burial vault that's being planned at the new headquarters of NBZ.

Essentially, what separates the gourmet fundraising TV dinner from a Swanson TV dinner is that you eat a Swanson's in your bathrobe while a gourmet dinner calls for black tie. In addition, there are TV monitors all around the banquet hall—and better yet, live TV stars at every table.

Ms. Faux Pas can attest to that. Though she is not a TV star yet, by an amazing coincidence Ms. Faux Pas received an invitation to one of these dinners that seemed to be intended for Miss Fawn Hallmark, the TV luminary and spokesperson for Shredded Wheaties. Ms. Faux Pas considered sending back the invitation, but for the good of her country she decided to just follow orders and show up at the Museum of Networking TV Dinner honoring the Joan Tom-Collins Divorce Proceedings Special, the Iran-Contradictory Hearings, and the Have-a-Nice-Day Awards, which salute the sign-off styles of anchorpersons. Ms. Faux Pas was seated by chance between Oliver North-by-northwest and Dan Rathernot, the courageous anchorperson who once crossed an angry home knitters' picket line and recently claimed to have been ambushed on Park Avenue by a Geraldo Herrera look-alike. Luckily Ms. Faux Pas had brought along Bubbly Waters's dinner party guide: "How to Make Small Talk with Practically Any Celebrity About Practically Anything."

Of course, glitterati parties have rituals that take the anxiety out of small talk. You talk left for five minutes and then talk right for five more. In that time you can hardly get beyond the status-establishing questions: name, hair-dresser, decorator, and what floor your apartment is on (higher is better, *chéries*). When it was time to talk left, Ollie, as he begged to be called, was so helpful, recommending the best little tire shops and hosiery discount stores in Central America. Dan Rathernot was a little imposing at first, until Ms. Faux Pas, following Bubbly Waters's rule of defensive conversation, apologized for what she was about to ask him and then bluntly asked why he couldn't get along with his boss, that nice Larry Trisch, who was sitting at the next table between Vanna Whitebread and the Flying Nun. Before he could answer, the M.C. said, "Let's go to the videotape."

With that, Ms. Faux Pas et al tilted back in their Lazy-guy reclining dining chairs as the waiters passed Paul Blue-Eyes's gourmet popcorn.

Unfortunately, some people just can't sit still when there's a TV set turned on. No sooner had the videotape begun to roll than glitterati around the room started getting up and going to the refrigerator, thoughtfully brought in for the occasion.

When his five minutes of small talk with Ms. Faux Pas were up, Dan Rathernot leaned over to Oliver North-by-northwest and whispered: "Forgive me for asking this, but what have you done with the smoking gun?"

Ollie thanked Dan for giving him the opportunity to answer that question and recited the Marine Corp instructions for handling smoking guns. Then he gave Ms. Faux Pas his unfinished bag of Nicaraguan nachos and excused himself, saying he had to go to the opening of Farewell to Arms Dealers, a new Iranian restaurant owned by a former colleague.

As Ollie bent to pick up his briefcase in the darkened room, his medals got tangled in the chain of Ms. Faux Pas's evening bag and knocked it to the floor. Apparently, in the ensuing disentanglement, a small box from Ollie's briefcase found its way into Ms. Faux Pas's bag—a fact she discovered only after he left, when she reached into her bag for Bubbly Waters's guidebook. It was a videocassette labeled Smoking Gun. Uh, oh. Ms. Faux Pas is no dummy. She knows that during the Iran-Contradictory affair everyone was looking for the smoking gun—the proof that the president knew what he knew when he forgot it, in spite of the fact that he forgot it when he really didn't know it. Dan, whose ratings were slipping, would kill for this tape.

What would that great patriot Fawn Hallmark have done in this situation? But of course! If Fawn couldn't make Shredded Wheaties out of it, she'd have smuggled it out of the room in her blouse, *n'est-ce pas*? Ms. Faux Pas wouldn't mind the spoils of smuggling—getting one's own William Morrisson agent and a twenty-six-week contract as a talk show host. Voilà! Ms. Faux Pas slipped the tape into her blouse and excused herself.

Smoking Gun has been an entertaining addition to Ms. Faux Pas's video library—in the closet. When a congressional committee came by asking questions a few weeks after the TV dinner, Ms. Faux Pas served them some nachos and screened the tape, explaining it was a pilot episode of *Smoking Gun*, a new TV spy series. The committee thought that Ronnie Reaganomics deserved an Ollie, a new award for believability, for his performance. The case was closed. *Vraiment!*

The next time she sees you, Ms. Faux Pas will tell you how to order a patented Fawn Hallmark blouse with a large hidden pocket in the back— please specify letter or legal size.

Gossip Patrol

Pass the water pistol, *s'il vous plait*, so Ms. Faux Pas can dampen the spirits of her rival manners columnists. Now that it's fashionable to feud in public, Ms. Faux Pas has a few people to whom she'd like to send a Dear Rodent letter. "Dear Rodent" is how Suzy Q, the Queen of Gossip, addressed *News-a-day-late* columnist Jamie Riviera after

he blabbed to *tout le monde* that, based on the account Suzy Q gave of a certain nouvelle society party at the Metaphysical Museum, either she needed new bifocals or she wasn't at the party at all. Jamie definitely was there, and he was particularly incensed that Suzy Q's column incorrectly placed his relative by marriage, Lana Riviera, at the soigné soiree in a *long* dress, when anyone who doesn't have to wait for a table at Mort Mortenson's *knows* that the leggy Lana hasn't worn a long dress since the day of her wedding to the late eye-shadow king, Chaz Riviera.

Pauvre Suzy Q was caught between a rock and a hard roll. Obviously, no woman *d'un certain age* is going to admit she needs ocular augmentation. It was easier for her to let everyone assume she got the guest list wrong because she wasn't at the party. The feud between these two gossips got so nasty that righteous Jamie petitioned his congressman to draft a truth-in-gossip law, which prompted the Prolific Prize committee to take gossip out of the Fiction category and put it in News Reporting—a move that most people agree will doom gossip to be as poorly read as funeral parlor ads.

Rather than wait for remedial legislation, a group of glitterati, who claim to be fed up with reading in gossip columns that they were seen the night before at parties they wouldn't be caught dead at, organized the GVs—the Gossip Vigilantes. It's the GVs' duty to verify the who, what, when, and where—but never the why—of major social events. "It's a tough-chic job, but somebody has to do it," says John Fairweather, the socially concerned publisher of *WWWW*, the stock market guide to the ups and downs of women's hemlines.

Anyone who can't get a table at Mort Mortenson's (and Ms. Faux Pas counts herself among them) must admit that going to a party as a Gossip Vigilante is the next best thing to reading about it when you unwrap the fish. Ms. Faux Pas would never have dreamt of *volunteering* for the job of GV; however, due to a series of misadventures, she recently found herself *drafted* for gossip patrol at the wedding of the year.

It all started in Bloomingberg's lower depths, where Ms. Faux Pas was buying a newly statusy *faux* car phone, when she took a wrong turn, and, pushed along by the crowd, ended up on a silver-bullet subway car headed for trendy SoSo, the gentrification capital of the world. Even the IRT was getting gentrified, mused Ms. Faux Pas, as she followed her nose to a cloud of expensive-smelling *eau de parfum*. Unexpectedly, her fragrant fellow travelers were a dozen Cornelia Gueststar look-alikes. They were on their way, it turned out, to a bridal shower for bride-of-the-year Lorelei Steinburger (the two-silver-spoons-in-the-mouth daughter of takeover mogul Sunny Steinburger), who was marrying *up* to the three-silver-spoon motel tycoon, handsome Jonathan Trisch, on the following Monday.

Admittedly, Monday is an unusual day for a glitterati wedding, but apparently it was (a) the groom's day off; (b) the only day five hundred glitterati weren't otherwise engaged; and (c) the Help's Day Off at the Metaphysical Museum, where the wedding bacchanal was being held. But back to the IRT.

The debs, most of whom had never been on a subway before, except in Moscow, were being escorted by a brigade of vigilantes in rather stunning fuchsia berets: not Gossip Vigilantes, to be sure, but a band of the notorious Guardian Anglers, so called because they are frequently fishing for publicity.

Drawn to the *faux* phone, one of the burly Anglers struck up a conversation with Ms. Faux Pas, and before you could say Radical Chic, he had convinced her to trade her phone for his millinery.

Clothes do make the woman. Looking properly vigilant now, Ms. Faux Pas struck up a conversation with the debs, and, when her knowledge of glitterati nightlife became apparent, she was invited by one of the fragrant group to be Gossip Vigilante at the newsworthy wedding. In anticipation of the Great Day, the bride gave Ms. Faux Pas a lovely gold pen engraved with the wedding logo—Just a Small Family Wedding of the Year—and took her shoe size for the complimentary two new pairs of shoes that all members of the wedding party were entitled to—one for going down the aisle, the other for going up.

It would be Ms. Faux Pas's job to verify the guest list and leak it to the top gossips—Suzy Q, Jamie Riviera, Billy Greenwich, and Liz Smithereens. But this was easier said than done. Apparently the wedding was not the hottest ticket in town, even though it was being held on a convenient Monday. Many of the people invited weren't thrilled with the dress code: White Tie and New Shoes—but who can blame the hostess, resourceful Glad-Fred Steinburger. She was carpeting the museum for one night and she wanted some afterlife for the white rug, which she planned to use to carpet the beach in Easthampton. Ms. Faux Pas was unhappy to discover that Princess Fruggie had defected; after reading that morning's *WWWW*, she decided a trip to Paris to have all her skirts lengthened was more important. Princess To-Die-For sent last-minute regrets saying she couldn't cancel her dirty dancing lesson. Stargazers Ronnie and Nancy Reaganomics canceled on the advice of their astrologer, who said their stars would be in the wrong house that night. And Donald and Ilana Trumpet, two of the biggest drawing cards in town, said they were going to a book signing.

Obviously, the list would be much more interesting with a little creative tampering, but if righteous Jamie Riviera got wind that Princess To-Die-For or Donald Trumpet weren't *really* at the wedding, Ms. Faux Pas would never be able to count heads at a party again.

In case Suzy Q is interested, the solution was simple, at least for Ms. Faux Pas. She got permission to invite Patrick Sways-a-lot, the dirty dancer. Then she left a message at the palace saying if Princess To-Die-For liked dancing with John Revolta, she'd love Patrick Sways-a-lot. Ilana Trumpet was lured with an option on the bridegroom's Park Avenue motel, on the condition that she bring Donald to the wedding. The hardest job was convincing Crystal Ball, the Reaganomicses' astrologer, to find something in the stars that would make a presidential appearance auspicious. The promise of a job for Ronnie Reaganomics as weatherman next year at the bridegroom's uncle's radio station, and, for Crystal Ball, a contract for her own Dial-a-Psychic show finally did the job. And Princess Fruggie was hooked with an offer of a complete wardrobe with unlimited hemline adjustments by Scarcely, the one-name Manhattan couturier to the glitterati. All the glits came of course—in new shoes, to boot. *Absolutment!* And Princess To-Die-For caught the bride's bouquet. It should make a nice boutonniere for the Prince. Care to check it out, Jamie?

The next time she sees you, Ms. Faux Pas will tell you what Donald Trumpet said when he tried to use the Guardian Angler's faux *car phone.*

II

Fashion

The New Handbag
Competition:
Going for the Gold

Tell the driver to wait, please. Ms. Faux Pas is having trouble squeezing everything into her minaudière. (In case you don't *parlez français*, that's a small metal evening bag that's really a box that's really a must in nouvelle society, and it had better be the real thing, because the other minaudière owners pride themselves on detecting the fakes.)

Ms. Faux Pas wishes someone would please tell the minaudière purveyors, who do a land-office business in $15,000-and-up solid-gold melon-shaped bags, that Ms. Faux Pas cannot fit all the emergency equipment of social life into her petite gold-and-diamond cantaloupe.

Perhaps in the twenties, when the clutch bag was transformed into precious jewelry, all a lady needed for a night on the town was lipstick, a compact, and mad money. But today, social security requires nothing less than a diamond-studded steamer trunk to hold one's business cards, lorgnette, Krazy Glue, walkie-talkie, French-English dictionary, contact-lens case, corkscrew, extra buttons, quarters for phone calls to one's answering machine, jeweler's loupe, and all the goody bags they hand out at parties these days.

Ms. Faux Pas's friend Holly GoSlowly, who is terribly nearsighted, is so short of space in her frog-shaped pavé-diamond minaudière that she's having the frog retrofitted to wear her contact lenses when she takes them off. Then the bulky lens case can be left at home.

The minaudières were out in force for the recent opening of the Metaphysical Museum's Costume Party Institute exhibit of the History of Handbags. Anyone who didn't have a proper minaudière bought one for the event. While most people believe the purpose of the Costume Institute's parties is for the ladies to check out each other's gowns, the real interest is in minaudières, which are to glitterati what tiaras are to royalty.

As everyone knows, glitterati ladies do not eat in public. And one of the things that helps pass the time at social dinners is appraising the other minaudières on the table (the minaudière should, incidentally, be placed in front of one's service plate—never to the side, where a waiter might put salad dressing on it). The sound of five hundred minaudières being plopped down on the table simultaneously is rivaled only by the thud of a thousand falling coconuts.

All conversation at the table stopped when Mercedes Beaucoup, the socialite Persian bombshell, nonchalantly placed her handsome new bejeweled evening bag on the table. The four other women at the table reached for their loupes. A description of Mercedes's minaudière (tapped out in code on the wineglasses) sped through the Met's Water Fountain Room. The minaudière was, of course, a gift from Mercedes's intended, billionaire Sam Trout, the Texas catch of the day, and it was shaped like a fish, for obvious reasons.

Not to be outdone, Lana Riviera, widow of the eyeliner king, had gotten her minaudière out of the vault for the occasion. Lana's is shaped like a shark cage, which makes it a little awkward to clutch while dancing—but it has the advantage over the rounded-bottom variety of not sliding off the table during the dinner and breaking the toes of the long-suffering Ingenious Food waiters.

You have to pack your minaudière pretty early in the morning to outdo Broke Faster, the swinging philanthropist. She was so tired of opening and closing her minaudière at parties for all the people with their hands out for handouts that she asked banker J. D. Rockefella to convert her minaudière into an automatic-teller cash machine. Mrs. Faster gave a Gold Card with unlimited withdrawal privileges to Gregorian Chanterelle, president of the New York Notorious Library.

Interestingly, Women with Minaudières, a newly powerful women's group, has managed to accomplish what a decade of radical feminists couldn't—to put a stop to the barbaric custom of women adjourning to the drawing room after dinner while the men linger over brandy and cigars. Although the Other Etiquette Adviser (as Ms. Faux Pas prefers to call her competitor, whom Ms. Faux Pas never mentions by name) forbids touching up makeup at the dinner table, Ms. Faux Pas has noticed that even otherwise well-mannered glitterati can't resist sneaking a peek in the mirrors of their precious handbags. Once Pandora's *boîte* is opened, it's nearly impossible to get it shut due to metal fatigue, dented edges (from being dropped so often), and overloading. *Serious* overloading.

Look at Vickie Forlorn's minaudière. Vickie, wife of the necktie mogul Ralph Forlorn, always carries her husband's spare pair of jeans in her minaudière in case the pair he lives in should suddenly disintegrate.

Gwendolyne Chrome Krevisse, the upwardly mobile designer of tall-gals clothing and a self-improvement buff, has a tape deck built into her minaudière with a continuous-loop elocution tape so that she can work on her diction whenever there's a lull in the conversation.

Francophile Suzi Richfriend stuffs her French-English dictionary into her talking minaudière, which pronounces *"formidable"* every time Suzi presses the catch.

Socialite-publisher Ann Go-Getter, an avid reader who is always on the move, keeps a copy of *The Naked Lunch Box* (which she published but has never read to the end) in her minaudière and throws away the pages as she finishes them. She'll have to read faster to make room for her new necessity—a walkie-talkie. Ann bought one the morning after the Met's History of Handbags opening night, which has come to be known as Limousine Gridlock Night because of a sudden snowstorm that made it impossible for anyone to find his own car and driver. Ms. Faux Pas wasn't too proud to take a cab, but nearsighted Holly GoSlowly hopped into a limo other than her own. James, the driver, never noticed, since Mrs. Go-Getter, his employer, carries the same gold-and-diamond frog minaudière as Holly does. Poor Mrs. Go-Getter. She had to hitch a ride home with a woman who carried a so-so satin evening bag.

Alas, Limousine Gridlock Night was the last time Holly got any mileage out of her minaudière. The following week at dinner at Gwendolyne and Harry Krevisse's, the nearsighted Holly was eyeballing a Ming dish when one of the Fabergé eggs on her charm bracelet smashed a shard out of the side of it.

(Please don't tell Gwendolyne and Harry.) Holly quickly pulled a tiny tube of Krazy Glue from her minaudière, repaired the damage, and dropped the glue back into her bag. Unfortunately, she forgot to close the glue tube. She hasn't been able to open her minaudière since.

Sad to say, this means no dessert for Holly. Like many Women with Minaudières, Holly doesn't eat in the presence of others. She is in the habit of using her *boîte* as a stash, filling it at parties with canapés, petit fours, and chocolate-covered fruits like those passed out recently as guests were leaving a Creole Society dinner, open minaudières in hand.

Ms. Faux Pas shudders to think what a bunch of chocolate-covered grapes would do to a satin evening bag. The only problem with Ms. Faux Pas's new, enlarged minaudière is getting it in and out of the trunk of the car. Monsieur Bellhop, some assistance, *s'il vous plait.*

The next time she sees you, Ms. Faux Pas will tell you what happened when Gwendolyne Chrome Krevisse discovered the top of the Krazy Glue tube under the Ming dish.

April in Paris, in January

Excusez-moi, while Ms. Faux Pas puts you on hold. Ms. Faux Pas is recently back from Paris and *tout le monde* is calling to find out what's hot there. Not the weather, to be sure. That's because in Paris, April takes place in January, when the spring (and summer) haute couture collections are unveiled.

And although you may think the pouf skirt is hot, the pouf is getting cold—and it's all Ms. Faux Pas's fault.

You may wonder why Ms. Faux Pas, who buys her spring clothes—*après* the season—in the summer when they go on sale, would have intimate knowledge of the strange rituals of French haute couture, in which the price of a dress-for-success suit is equivalent to the annual starting salary for Harvard Business School graduates.

But due to an *incroyable* case of mistaken identity, Ms. Faux Pas was initiated into the mysteries of high fashion by a world-famous editor.

Actually, Ms. Faux Pas was already headed for Paris the economical way. She was standing in line at JFK with her Born to Shop the January Sales tour group—which was unfortunately overbooked—when she was miraculously upgraded to the Concorde.

When the attendant at the check-in counter asked to see Ms. Faux Pas's ticket, Ms. Faux Pas said, *"D'accord"* (which is what glitterati say instead of okay), and suddenly she was ushered into the Concorde lounge.

There she was befriended by none other than Belle d'Orsay, the longtime French fashion forecaster, who mistook Ms. Faux Pas for an American fashion editor because she was dressed all in black. (Ms. Faux Pas always wears black when she travels because she once read a book on style by Lana Riviera, widow of the nail-polish king, advising that in case the plane is diverted to Beirut because of the weather, a little black dress goes anywhere.)

Trying to look nonchalant in the Concorde lounge, Ms. Faux Pas was reading *Il & Elle*, the *Harvard Lampoon* fashion magazine. Madame d'Orsay asked Ms. Faux Pas if that was *her* magazine. Ms. Faux Pas replied, *"D'accord,"*

meaning it was her *copy*. Madame d'Orsay (who has had her share of misunderstandings—one of which resulted in her being barred for a time from couturier Yves Saint Honoré's fashion showings) misunderstood, assuming Ms. Faux Pas worked for *Il & Elle*, and offered to take her to the spring shows. *"D'accord,"* said Ms. Faux Pas, thinking it might be a good way to find some markdowns.

Pointing to the man across the aisle surrounded by white flower arrangements, Madame d'Orsay explained that the fashion world has its own orbit and doesn't revolve around the sun, but around its Sun King, the fashion forecaster Jean-Louis Fairweather. He is the publisher of *WWWW*—the Who, What, When, and Where (but never the Why) of fashion. In the trade, King Fairweather is referred to as "Louie Sez" because, depending on what he says in *WWWW*, a designer can take off like a meteor or become a falling star.

Since King Fairweather likes to spend September in New York in April, he decreed that April in Paris would be more convenient in January. Anyone who finds the fashion calendar confusing can read *WWWW* and learn how to make fashion predictions like a pro—that is, while being seasonally disoriented and jet-lagged.

The first requirement of a fashion forecaster, Madame d'Orsay confided, is to be able to attend a Paris runway show without getting claustrophobic. The exit crush at one of these events is so serious that fashion editors have been known to lock earrings and chain bags. Madame d'Orsay gave Ms. Faux Pas smelling salts and wire cutters for such emergencies, and lent her a chain bag to tote it all in.

The second rule of fashion forecasting, said Madame d'Orsay, is: In order to get a good seat at the showings, always wear something by the couturier. Obviously, with five or more shows per day, it makes sense for Belle d'Orsay to travel around in a Citroën dressing room on wheels—and change in the van rather than return *chez elle* to do so.

Madame d'Orsay is known to be one of the world's best customers for haute couture. Only in the daytime will she dress off-the-rack. In the evening, she says, haute couture is a must, or else she feels just a little—how do you say it?—"cheap."

Ms. Faux Pas, who is definitely—how do you say it—"thrifty," hoped her collection of designer scarves would assure front-row seats. But as Madame d'Orsay pointed out, scarves don't count as homage, since couturiers don't always design their own. (Ms. Faux Pas is going to demand a refund from the street peddler at Fifty-ninth and Lexington.)

Anyway, once seated in the Grandiose Hotel ballroom, where the most prestigious couture shows are held, Belle d'Orsay (who had gotten Ms. Faux Pas a front-row seat) explained that the main preoccupation is not the show. All the important journalists have previewed the clothes so they can write their columns ahead of time. This allows them to note what the competition is wearing and figure out how to exit without locking earrings. Those in front can vault up on the runway and get out fast by following it backstage. The only drawback to this escape route is that one must pass the couturier, who is standing back there taking note of which editors are not wearing his designs.

"Why not just sit in your seat till the ballroom empties out?" asked the naive Ms. Faux Pas.

"So you can dash to the Hotel Ritzy before the others and see who's arriving with whom for lunch." *D'accord.*

But fashion forecasting is not all drudgery—working lunches, measuring the ebb and flow of hemlines, changing the water in the flowers one receives. In the evening, there's always a party. Were it not for Belle d'Orsay, Ms. Faux Pas would never have been invited to socialite Suzi Richfriend's annual surprise party.

The surprise is not for Suzi. It's for the guests, who never know in advance where the party will take place. They assemble on the roof of the Ritzy and are whisked by helicopter to an unexpected mise-en-scène. The guests were delighted that this year Suzi chose a place closer than last year's venue on top of the Matterhorn, where all the guests ruined their shoes in the snow.

This year Suzi staged a gala dinner-dance for five hundred chums in the grand foyer of the Paris Light Opera House. It was preceded by a fashion showing of highlights of the couture season. Belle d'Orsay had a serious which-couturier-to-pay-homage-to problem. She settled for shoes, gown, wrap, brooch, chapeau, and petticoat, each by a different couturier. Ms. Faux Pas had no choice. She piled the scarves on her little black dress. As she was fighting her way to her seat, Ms. Faux Pas found that her dress was hooked by a chain bag belonging to a reporter from *WWWW*. In the ensuing disentanglement, Ms. Faux Pas's dress sustained an embarrassing rip.

She considered running out to Belle d'Orsay's van for a change of wardrobe, but realized that Belle was wearing *everything* in the van. So Ms. Faux Pas fled to the ladies' room. The attendant offered to close the gap with twenty safety pins (chicly unconcealed), but Ms. Faux Pas recalled Belle saying, "The bag-lady look is *fini*."

One of the ushers offered Ms. Faux Pas his jacket and belt, but she remembered that *WWWW* had decreed the tough-chic look *fini* as well.

Finally the helpful attendant unlocked the door of a nearby opera dressing room, where Ms. Faux Pas spotted the perfect frock. The attendant made some adjustments. Voilà.

The show had already started. As Ms. Faux Pas returned to her seat, all eyes were on her. Had she chosen the wrong "look"? *Pas du tout.* Suddenly the photographers turned away from the models and started snapping Ms. Faux Pas in her poufed and panniered flowered silk Marie Antoinette gown. So *à la mode*. Long in back and, thanks to the adjustments, *très* short in front. Ms. Faux Pas was the only person in the place, except for the models, wearing the season's recherché costume-party look.

Noticing her for the first time, Jean-Louis Fairweather tossed one of his ubiquitous white bouquets her way. Would she care to make a statement for *WWWW*?

She was beginning to feel almost as powerful as a bona fide fashion forecaster. "It's time for fun in fashion, *n'est-ce pas?*" said Ms. Faux Pas authoritatively.

Perhaps too authoritatively. Madame d'Orsay leaned over to Mr. Fairweather conspiratorially and whispered, "I think the pouf is just about *fini, n'est-ce pas?*"

"*D'accord*," he responded with a sly smile. The next day, before Suzi Richfriend and her friends had even placed their orders, the death of the pouf and its imminent markdown was front page in *WWWW. Vraiment!*

The next time she sees you, Ms. Faux Pas will tell you what WWWW said when the powder-room attendant announced she was opening her own couture house.

III

Celebrities

Down But Not Out in Beverly Hills

P*ardon le* pinky, but Ms. Faux Pas has trouble shaking hands when her nails are wet. Ever since her recent trip to Beverly Hills, where she went to observe the lifestyles of the rich and infamous, her nails have frequently been wet. In that fabled city, the beauty salon is one of the few places where the ladies who won't lunch can chew what little fat is left with one another. Although the streets of Los Angeles are deserted, the status beauty salons are filled with gregarious women pretending to need manicures so they can find someone to talk to while keeping their hands out of the cookie jar. Some Beverly Hills women are so starved for human contact (not to mention Oreos) that they have their hair done every day. But because it's not easy to hear the latest Liz Customtailor-Malcolm Fourbits gossip while under the dryer, the frequent manicure has become the grooming ritual of preference.

By the time the nails are dry, it's time for dinner—but obviously no woman with three fresh coats of Raquel Red is going to cook, even if she knew how. In L.A., a favorite place to take one's nails to dinner is a charity ball. Benefits are popular because they're the only events in town at which the diamonds are larger than the rhinestones—and besides, you don't have to wait for a table. Ms. Faux Pas knows all this firsthand because of a chance encounter.

While doing research in a beauty salon on the folkways of the region, having her nails extended and polished in the native fashion, Ms. Faux Pas was befriended by a Beverly Hills wife with "million-dollar" nails, which in this neck of the woods means they are insured against breakage by Floyd's of London and have their own trust fund.

Whether it was Ms. Faux Pas's new, improved nails that did it, or her rich lode of Malcolm Fourbits anecdotes, before you could say, "No moons, please," she was invited to join the Beverly Hills wife and her husband at a dinner in support of a cause dear to the hearts—and heart-shaped necklines—of Hollywood: Save the Gowns.

As in other parts of the nation, historic preservation is alive and well in L.A.—although in this exotic culture what's preserved tends to be movie-star gowns, not movie-star homes. Even such historic buildings as the Homey Hills mansion of the late Bing Crossmyheart (the star who died so long ago, he never made a guest appearance on *The Love Boat*) are expendable if oil is struck below them or if some mogul wants to knock the house down to build a bigger one with twinned screening rooms, a multilevel parking garage, a mock diamond mine for the kids to dig in, and an environmentally safe incinerator for burning rejected screenplays—which *le tout* Hollywood seems to have trouble disposing of.

Each to his own, says Ms. Faux Pas, pretending she's a participant-observer in Samoa.

What to wear to the benefit was a more pressing issue. Actually, Ms. Faux Pas is an ardent believer in preserving gowns, although the urge isn't entirely historically certifiable. In the circles in which she travels, the well-dressed ladies take great pride in their personal clothes closets, often giving tours of them. Since no self-respecting glitterata can risk having her closet appear understocked, clothes ripe for the resale shop are often saved to fill the empty rods, even when one has no intention of wearing them again.

This custom is not to be confused with the Hollywood habit of buying books by the yard with no intention of reading them. New Yorkers buy books by the yard to appear erudite. In Hollywood, buying books by the yard is considered a patriotic act. For environmental reasons, the dumping and burning of the film capital's massive output of unaccepted screenplays has to be regulated. And what better use for the stacks of discarded works than bookcasefill.

Clever Candice Spellbinder, one of the most enterprising of Hollywood wives, went into business recently buying up all the scrap screenplays from the studios, binding them attractively in leather, and reselling them by the yard to Hollywood moguls. If only Candice would sell Ms. Faux Pas one of the many dresses hanging idly by the yard in Candice's closet. Most were designed for Candice by couturier-to-the-stars Nolandarling.

But Ms. Faux Pas was not totally without resources. In anticipation of attending a glitterati swap meet, she had brought along one of her surplus gowns—her pink satin prom dress—which she hoped to swap for something that would have more hanger appeal during closet tours.

Alas, when she returned with her new nails to the bungalow at the Beverly Hillbillies Hotel to dress for dinner, the old prom dress was lying in a heap on the floor of the closet. No problem, said Clark, the charming valet (an aspiring screenwriter and, after hours, a screenplays-by-the-yard salesman for Mrs. Spellbinder). He promised to have the dress pressed in a flash, while Ms. Faux Pas was having her makeup done by Garth (another aspiring screenwriter).

But as soon as the freshly made-up Ms. Faux Pas returned to her closet, she realized there was a problem. Clark had somehow gotten things mixed up. The wrong dress was on the hanger. It was white and pleated. This wasn't Ms. Faux Pas's prom dress. It was someone else's and not bad-looking at that. *C'est la vie*, said Ms. Faux Pas, as she quickly slipped into it, vowing to report the mix-up to the valet the next day.

Because of California's tough seat-belt laws, after Ms. Faux Pas arrived at the ball in the vintage Thunderbird she had rented from an aspiring screenwriter, she had to spend the first half of the evening in the ladies' room blow-drying the seat-belt strap marks out of her rented sable wrap. By the time she took her seat in the ballroom between yet another aspiring screenwriter and her host, the Hollywood husband, the Save the Gowns fashion show was about to begin.

The philanthropic members of Les Dames de la Hollywood Closet had raised enough money to restore Theda Barry's ankle bracelet, Jean Crawford's first pair of shoulder pads, Mae Westerly's whalebone corset, the demure costume Joan Tom-Collins wore to the hearing for her divorce from Peter Homely, and, *quel coup*—the fringed purple leather motorcycle jacket with matching helmet that Liz Custom-tailor wore for dirt-biking with Malcolm Four-bits.

Just as Liz was making a surprise entrance

on her lavender motorcycle, the spotlight suddenly shifted to Ms. Faux Pas. There must be some mistake, she whispered to the screenwriter on her right as *le tout* Hollywood gave her a standing ovation. "Your dress—it's the long-lost peekaboo dress worn by Marilyn Monrose in the *Seven Year Hitch*," he shouted, as Ms. Faux Pas was propelled to center stage. Out of the corner of her eye she saw Clark, the valet, holding her misplaced prom dress and waving it frantically.

But he was too late. Ms. Faux Pas was beginning to understand the saying, Clothes make the woman. Just one minute in Marilyn Monrose's pleats and already Ms. Faux Pas could feel a transformation taking place. "So this is what it feels like to go Hollywood," she said to herself.

Blowing a kiss to Clark, the valet, she demanded petulantly: "Darling, please call Ms. Faux Pas's agent and say Ms. Faux Pas has a great idea for a screenplay—can her agent get her a two-picture deal? Then call Nolandarling and tell him Ms. Faux Pas needs six new gowns by tomorrow. And put the manicurist on standby in the Poloshirt Lounge. If a certain star doesn't move her motorcycle, Ms. Faux Pas may lose a nail scratching out someone's violet eyes. And please, Clark, darling—get rid of that tacky dress you're holding—*pronto!*"

The next time she sees you, Ms. Faux Pas will introduce her new fragrance, Un Succès Fou, which, according to Liz Customtailor, is "the best perfume."

Confessions of a
Temp for
Donald Trumpet

Bonjour tristesse! Please tell Howard Reubensandwich, the power publicist, that Ms. Faux Pas will be late for their meeting to discuss her book tour. She can't go anywhere until she crosses the many T's in her juicy memoir of her days as a consultant to Donald Trumpet, the celebrity builder. Joni Evensteven, the power publisher, is imploring Ms. Faux Pas to finish the book *toute suite* because today any book with *Trumpet* in the title can sell a million. Ms. Faux Pas doesn't want to be scooped by Donald's chauffeur, Donald's pilot, Donald's marble cutter, and the kindergarten teacher who had Donald junior in her class—all of whom are writing their own Donald Trumpet books.

Little did Ms. Faux Pas realize several years ago, when Fugit Temps, the employment agency, sent her to fill in for a vacationing Trumpette—one of Donald's many secretaries—that the shy Donald would one day boast a walk-on in a Judi Frantz movie, make it onto the best-seller list, and get thousands of prominent people to shake hands with him on the receiving line at his Book Party of the Year.

In those days, when Ms. Faux Pas was just typing around, it never crossed her mind that she would one day be the image and etiquette adviser to the Nouveau Rich and Famous.

When she first met Mr. Trumpet, he was already on his way to being an artist-dealmaker. His only problem was that his pizzazz quotient was low. He was perceived as unimaginative—he wore a different color tie every day, did deals over lunch, and flew on commercial airlines like any run-of-the-mill mogul.

At the risk of blowing her own trumpet (something she was eventually able to teach Donald to do eminently well), Ms. Faux Pas believes the Donald Trumpet story might have had a different ending if, one evening, she hadn't volunteered to work late. Of course, you'd never know any of this from reading Donald's book.

C'est la vie. Ms. Faux Pas will set the record straight in her own book, which begins on that fateful evening when the smart kid from Queens let down his golden hair, so to speak, after Ms. Faux Pas questioned why he wanted her to sign his letters, "Your obedient servant, D. Trumpet."

Ms. Faux Pas said that sounded anonymous and obsequious. He admitted it probably mirrored his mood. "Nobody knows my name except the cement contractors and my bank loan officer," he complained. "Harry Helmsleona is building a palace, and I don't even have a mansion in the Hamptons—only a gamekeeper's cottage. What am I doing wrong?"

First of all, said Ms. Faux Pas, you've got to stop using concrete. Use marble instead. It's classier. Then, stop getting your money from banks and start getting it from investors who give interesting dinner parties. Forget about building apartment houses in Queens. If you want to be somebody, rescue a landmark—like that old boarded-up hotel near Grand Central Terminal. "And Donald," she admonished, "get rid of the military school haircut and let your hair touch your collar."

The rest is history. With the backing of some wealthy Chicagoans who give interesting dinner parties, Donald marbleized the old Commadorable Hotel to much acclaim. The increased traffic also helped the neighboring railroad company, which was so grateful for the boost, it asked Donald if he'd like to marbleize its aging West Side railroad yards, which were looking a bit dowdy.

Donald asked Ms. Faux Pas what she thought of his idea of establishing a superkindergarten there, since he was having trouble finding a proper school for his kids.

"No, Donald, think bigger. Build a city within a city. To get a lot of publicity on TV, call it TV Sitcom City. But first create a marbleized tourist attraction—a vertical shopping mall on Fifth Avenue. You might want to run for national office one day, and tourists will remember the builder who gave them marbleized rest rooms."

Donald was truly grateful for the idea, and as everyone knows, he built the Marble Mall, as he had hoped to call it until Ms. Faux Pas vetoed the name.

"Then I'll call it Robert Tower, after my brother," said the self-effacing Donald. But Ms. Faux Pas prevailed, and Donald reluctantly accepted her suggestion to call the building Trumpet Tower. It was a great success, although the tourists didn't do all that much shopping. But Donald's wife, Ilana, bought enough there to keep the stores in the black. Now many people know Donald Trumpet's name, and he has gotten to like the attention (and the power dinner parties).

Noticing the beginning of a paunch, Ms. Faux Pas suggested some conspicuous austerity—giving up lunch. "Take only tomato juice," she told him. "And wear only red ties, so if you spill the juice it won't show."

All that was needed now was a way to keep Donald in the papers. Publicity, as he has said, is very useful when you're making deals. Ms. Faux Pas suggested a feud with a powerful government official, preferably one who also needed publicity. A deal was struck with the mayor of New York that was beneficial to both parties.

Next, Ms. Faux Pas suggested that Donald propose erecting the world's tallest building at TV Sitcom City, one that would put all the skyscrapers in the world to shame. But when Donald announced the deal, the mayor, playing his role too well, objected, saying the tower would cast a large shadow over his administration, which had enough shadows over it already.

If Donald could solve this problem, Ms. Faux Pas told him, everyone in the world would know his name. Donald went out on the terrace of his penthouse at Trumpet Tower with his portable phone. When he returned, he had a very self-satisfied smile on his face. He said he had just spoken to the cardinal (whom he had met at an interesting dinner party), and the cardinal had just spoken to someone higher up—and it was a done deal: it would cost a pretty penny, but for six months of the year, the sun would rise in the west and set in the east, thus casting the shadow of TV Sitcom City Tower over Leonard Astern's competing development in New Jersey in the afternoon.

But perhaps Ms. Faux Pas has told you too much about her memoirs. Donald just offered her unlimited free shopping in Trumpet Tower to forget she ever worked for him. But she has taken an offer of cold cash from *That's Life* instead. As you always say, Donald, making deals is an art form.

The next time she sees you, the excruciatingly thin Ms. Faux Pas, who is rushing off to Christian Incroyable's for a fitting of her $24,995 dress, will explain why it's really not all that expensive to be rich. Think how much you save by having only V-8 for lunch.

IV

Trends

How to Worry
About Tomorrow Today

———

Take it from Ms. Faux Pas:

This month you're going to come into money—unless you came into it last month (finding a quarter in a pay phone counts).

You will be a guest on Bubbly Waters's show—or you will watch it.

You will receive a valentine from a handsome person—or you will send one.

The only thing that can be predicted with certainty is that you will pay $75 for this advice.

Please excuse Ms. Faux Pas for not getting up, but she is going to take this meeting lying down. She got some worrisome news last week

———

from her intuitive counselor. (An intuitive counselor, in case you've been out of town for the weekend, is the New Age term for a psychic—and this month, at least, everybody who's anybody swears by ICs.) Ms. Faux Pas's buddy, girl-about-town Tammy Rupert, got Ms. Faux Pas her hard-to-get appointment with the intuitive counselor. "A good IC is cheaper than a shrink," says Tammy, "because ICs get to the point faster and don't insist on talking about your mother."

Ms. Faux Pas's intuitive counselor was cheaper than an orthopedist. The IC said she had a sixth sense that Ms. Faux Pas recently had—or was on the verge of having—back trouble. (Unlike shrinks and orthopedists, intuitive counselors, it seems, often get the past and future mixed up. This may be confusing to the client, but it has the happy side effect of doubling the counselor's chances of being right.)

Actually, Ms. Faux Pas can list several people who give her a pain in the neck—or are soon going to—but she must confess her sacroiliac hasn't kicked up since the back-breaking dinner party at decorator Lothario Frittata's, when everyone sat on the floor on chintz pillows.

Even though she's pain-free now and a confirmed chair user, Ms. Faux Pas is taking no chances. Her intuitive counselor, Crystal Ball, has an amazing track record—or is going to. She did her training with Esmerelda Superpower (everyone calls her ESP), a psychic who,

at age five, was certified clairvoyant by Duke and Duchess University, which gives degrees in Out-of-Body Experience. Miss Ball and ESP work around the clock for country-and-western stars and corporate nabobs, and every few months these intuitive ladies take their auras, vibes, and hunches to the Big Apple for a week and place them at the disposal of the glitterati—of whom Ms. Faux Pas is one, or soon will be.

One prerequisite for being a glitterata is having complete faith in the pronouncements of intuitive counselors, astrologers, numerologists, and junk-bond brokers. Most of the designers Ms. Faux Pas is dressed by will not reach for a pin unless their numerologists tell them how many to pick up. And the last fashion show Ms. Faux Pas attended was called for exactly 7:21 p.m. because that was the previous week's lottery number. These seem extreme measures to take in order to avoid talking about your mother, but to each his own.

Ms. Faux Pas knew she was on her way to the Glitterati Hall of Fame when she passed Ivan Boyscout, the well-known arbitrageur, who is in trouble, or is going to be, coming out of Tammy Rupert's pied-à-terre as Ms. Faux Pas was going in for her IC appointment. Tammy lets ESP and Crystal Ball operate from her flat when they come to town. Tammy doesn't mind the wear and tear on her floor pillows, but she thinks the counselors ought to be a bit more intuitive about how many candles they'll need and bring them along instead of burning all of hers.

The skeptical Ms. Faux Pas had vowed to remain inscrutable during her intuitive counseling session and not offer more information about herself than necessary. Thus, Crystal Ball would be forced to prove her clairvoyance. But in a flash, Miss Ball had Ms. Faux Pas under her spell. Miss Ball examined the lines in Ms. Faux Pas's palm, glimpsed her aura, and announced: "You must stop and smell the flowers more."

Incredible! How did Miss Ball know Ms. Faux Pas hadn't smelled the flowers since designer José de la Rascal's perfume gave her an allergy attack? Ms. Faux Pas's skepticism was weakening.

Next, Miss Ball said: "A friend of yours is in trouble."

Uncanny! She must be referring to Ms. Faux Pas's buddy, *Daily Who's News* gossip columnist Billy Greenwich, who is feuding with José de la Rascal. Billy had to print an apology for pronouncing ruffles (José's strong suit) passé after José threatened to punch Billy in the nose.

Then Miss Ball said, "Help me out with this" (something she says quite frequently). She asked if Ms. Faux Pas had been to a party lately—or was going to one. And was she going to be wearing a coat?

Totally amazing! In fact, Ms. Faux Pas was on her way to Denny Whodunit's book-signing party at Mort Mortenson's Coat d'Azur, a favorite watering hole of the glitterati.

When Ms. Faux Pas got to Mortenson's Coat d'Azur that evening, she could barely get in the door. Half the mob were waiting to check their coats; the other half were waiting to claim their coats—which the attendants were ferrying to and from the coat "room," a blue stretch limousine parked out front.

After congratulating Denny Whodunit, Ms. Faux Pas tried to smell the flowers on the buffet table, but the pollen count in the room (glitterati all bathe in José de la Rascal's bath oil) was so high, she had an allergy attack and ended up smelling the potato pancakes instead.

Then Ms. Faux Pas bumped into Billy Greenwich, who was counting ruffled dresses. Ever since Billy got in hot water for writing that ruffles were passé, José de la Rascal's devoted customers, such as Teeny Mahogany, editor of *Vanity Unfair*, and Lana Riviera, widow of the lip-gloss king, have been wearing ruffles and crinolines in a gesture of support for José. Fashion editors around the world have mistaken this act of social solidarity for a fashion trend.

Ms. Faux Pas suggested to Billy that until the ruffle action died down he should switch to writing about intuitive counseling, which she assured him was all the rage on Wall Street. Billy was skeptical.

When Mort Mortenson blinked the lights, Ms. Faux Pas joined the crush of people at the door clamoring for their coats. While she was waiting, she decided to try once more to smell the flowers. As she leaned over the bar for a sniff, she felt a terrible twinge in her sacroiliac.

Even though Ms. Faux Pas finds a bout of back trouble inconvenient, she is relieved to know that her $75 did not go up in smoke with Tammy's candles. The IC had predicted back trouble correctly. On the other hand, Ms. Faux Pas was fascinated to read in the *Times on My Hands* that arbitrageur Ivan Boyscout claims he is not guilty of insider trading. He insists he got all his stock tips from a clairvoyant on the Upper East Side who sits on floor pillows and burns candles. But the SEC says it can find no trace of any such person. Ms. Faux Pas says, "*Cherchez la IC.*"

The next time she sees you, Ms. Faux Pas will give you a forwarding address for Ivan Boyscout's greenmail. Keep it under your chapeau.

Esprit de Corpse:
The Drop-Dead Dinner
Party

Ms. Faux Pas used to believe that parties, though often a pain, are not matters of life and death. But she has changed her tune after the party she attended recently: a whodunit dinner—complete with a mock murder staged by a troupe of hired actors, an entertainment that is suddenly to die for.

Since Ms. Faux Pas can't always be the life of the party, she is all for any device that will revive some of the parties she's invited to. And a harmless whodunit is infinitely preferable to the latest rage in Britain—the mock-POW-camp weekend, where the fun is in escaping. (You think Ms. Faux Pas has made this up, but you are wrong!)

Still, murder à la carte is not as nouvelle as it may seem. Ever since Ms. Faux Pas was old enough to cut the joint of the chicken leg on the first try, she has known that a Park Avenue dinner party can be deadlier than a table at Dumberto's Clam House. No sooner do members of the social mafia kiss you on both cheeks than they are stabbing you in the back.

Perhaps this explains why Elsa Maison, the hostess with the mostest condos to sell, wears a beaded bullet-proof mermaid dress at her monthly power soirees. Thus protected, she can waft among her guests with the same sense of security that underwater photographers have in their shark-proof cages.

Not that Elsa is above toying with her razor-toothed chums. As the guests arrive, Elsa's daughter, Romantique, hands out table-assignment cards shaped like Moorish daggers. Then the seating chart is passed, along with the hors d'oeuvres.

You are probably wondering how Ms. Faux Pas made it to one of Elsa Maison's legendary bashes, since Ms. Faux Pas is not an anchor-woman, a society woman, a princess, or in the market for a penthouse. But Ms. Faux Pas *is* public-spirited, and she won two invitations to the party in a five-dollar-a-chance Friends of the Manhattan Bridge Club raffle.

Elsa Maison, who is chairman of the fund-raising drive to save bridge (not the Manhattan Bridge, the *game* of bridge), a dying pursuit, raised $1 million in less than a week selling these chances. *Le tout* New York wants to be seen at one of Elsa Maison's parties—but only sixty-eight lucky glits can. Ms. Faux Pas's winning number made her glit for a night—which is much better than being queen for a day, she can assure you.

As her escort, Ms. Faux Pas invited the only man she knows with the proper clothes for Elsa Maison's (a tux with bulletproof cummerbund)—her old school chum, Denny Whodunit, the famous society mystery writer (*Murder in Trumpet Tower* and *Murder in the Concorde Lavatory*).

Ms. Faux Pas was delighted to learn that anchorpeople, socialites, and princesses are just as celebrity-mad as the rest of us. Everyone was autographing anchorman Dan Rathernot's cast while he was recounting how he had his leg broken on Park Avenue by two fashion authorities who hated his argyle vests. Decorators Billy Armoire and Lothario Frittata were comparing notes on which princesses, socialites, and anchorpersons are the slowest to pay; and Princess Irina Megalopolis, the Greco-Roman gold digger, was recruiting members for her new self-awareness cult, called Panning Out.

When Romantique hit the gong for dinner, Ms. Faux Pas took her seat between Rupert Puddlejumper, the Australian press lord, and Horst von Polo, the social walker.

After the soup, a bloodcurdling scream came from Ms. Faux Pas's table. It was Ms. Faux

Pas, who was screaming because she felt something warm and wet trickling on her open-toed Maude Frizons. A peek under the tablecloth revealed a woman's body—with a jeweled dagger in her back. It was Elsa Maison's astrologer—who charts Elsa's seating-of-the-stars by the stars.

Before you could say Hercule Poirot, dashing Denny Whodunit had taken charge. He said everyone present was a suspect. God knows, three of them had motives. Penny Puddlejumper, the press lord's wife, was furious at the astrologer for seating her in the Maisons' children's room with the bores and unknown spouses of the anchorpersons. Samantha Girly White, the radical feminist journalist, was still standing because she had refused her assigned seat on the other side of Horst von Polo, who is on trial for allegedly boring his wife to death. And Lothario Frittata had a grudge against Elsa because she used Billy Armoire to do her table decorations.

As the astrologer was carried away, Starling Leech, who was covering the party for *Lifestyles of the Rich and Shameless*, got out his camcorder and started shooting. In society, it doesn't matter what they accuse you of, as long as the pictures are good.

While Denny interrogated the suspects, the rest of the guests took a straw vote about who done it. But glitterati don't use straws. They use—what else?—knives. In society, as Ms. Faux Pas has learned, they never point when they're character assassinating. They leave the knife on the table and rotate it so the tip points toward the one who's being talked about. . . . Oh, my goodness, *all the knives are pointing at Ms. Faux Pas!*

Horst von Polo leaned over to Ms. Faux Pas and whispered "Don't worry, dear, I'll get you my lawyer."

Just at that moment, Elsa Maison stepped in and said, "Surprise! It's all a joke!" It was just the evening's entertainment: Homicide to Go.

As everyone knows, Elsa Maison believes that to be bored, for even a minute, is a fate worse than losing at bridge. And Ms. Faux Pas would be the first to agree that the evening involved no ennui.

While Ms. Faux Pas tried to recover her aplomb, Horst, as she was calling him by now, took her hand and gave her some advice. If she was going to live life in the expensive lane, there was only one thing she should know—something, he said, that he'd learned the hard way. "In this crowd," Horst said, "not being boring is a matter of life and death." Of corpse.

The next time she sees you, Ms. Faux Pas will tell you what happened after anchorperson Bubbly Waters, who arrived late, found out she'd been scooped by Dan Rathernot.

V

Arts & Letters

Walking Tall with the Literary Lions

Asseyez-vous while Ms. Faux Pas finishes standing on her head on the new tablecloth, and be careful not to slip on the hardwood floor's waxy buildup.

Ms. Faux Pas feels that she's expressing herself so much more now that she has an area rug on *top* of the dining table rather than under it.

Actually, Ms. Faux Pas had been contemplating putting a rug on the table for some time but didn't have the courage to express herself fully until overhearing at Arlo's, the florist to the glitterati, that the hors d'oeuvres table at the Pen & Pencil benefit at the Metro Club would be covered with a rug—the same rug that was under Jackie Suzanna's typing table when she wrote *Valley of the Barbie Dolls.*

Pen & Pencil, as you know, is the writer's organization that seeks Freedom of Expression for authors. The group's major coup to date was obtaining for Norman Mailman the right to say the f-word on *Good Morning North America.* Pen & Pencil also underwrote the Copy Editors' Conference at which it was unanimously decided that the word *billionaire* (which is turning up so frequently these days—especially in the minutes of the meetings of Pen & Pencil) should be spelled as it often is in the pages of *Timely* magazine—with a capital *B.*

Entre nous, Ms. Faux Pas was somewhat surprised at the choice of the Metro Club for a Freedom of Expression fundraiser, since expression is not one of the freedoms championed by the club—at least not when Ms. Faux Pas was there a while back. Even though Ms. Faux Pas adhered strictly to the club's dress code the last time she was a guest at an event there, her camera was rudely confiscated by the doorman. Rumor has it that cameras are banned at the Metro Club because club members fear some unauthorized person will smuggle out a photo of the Members in Arrears List.

Letting bygones be bygones, Ms. Faux Pas hoped she could pop into the party unnoticed, take a quick gander at the tablecloth under the hors d'oeuvres, and depart. But because of a misunderstanding, she ended up being mistaken for one of Pen & Pencil's most captivating Literary Lions.

Ms. Faux Pas's first mistake was to wear her Kritzia ballpoint pen on a chain around her neck. Little did Ms. Faux Pas realize that the Kritzia lion symbol and the Literary Lion lion symbol are almost identical—causing everyone to assume Ms. Faux Pas was a belle of *lettres.* Before she could cry Tom Wolfe, she was having her picture taken (by the Metro Club doorman) with everyone from writers Art Bookwall, Denny Whodunit, and Norman Mailman to *Vanity Unfair* editor Teeny Mahogany, philanthropist Broke Faster, library head Gregorian Chanterelle, Glad-Fred Steinburger (who, Ms. Faux Pas later discovered, was chairman of the event), and a tuxedoed Metro Club bartender, whom Ms. Faux Pas greeted with kisses on both cheeks, mistaking him for a glitterato.

Ms. Faux Pas wonders if other people are having as much trouble as she is lately in distinguishing the guests at parties from the well-dressed help, who are probably just Metro Club members working off their arrears.

Mistaking Mrs. Steinburger's secretary for Mrs. Steinburger was Ms. Faux Pas's next gaffe. Ms. Faux Pas should have known better, since everyone else seems to know that Glad-Fred Steinburger is a charter member of the Tall Gals Society, the philanthropic association of women over five feet six who are dedicated to doing good works by marrying

Billionaires (no matter what their height) and directing their charitable contributions. Mrs. Steinburger's secretary is of ordinary stature and therefore should never be mistaken for her boss or for other dedicated members of the Tall Gals—such as Gwendolyne Chrome Krevisse or Ilana Trumpet.

But the secretary made a gaffe of her own: she assumed from the novel under Ms. Faux Pas's arm—*Princess Maisie* by Judi Frantz—that Ms. Faux Pas was its author. *Au contraire*: Ms. Faux Pas is a Frantz fan and reads her religiously for shopping and decorating advice.

But once the name Judi Frantz had reverberated down the receiving line, the wrong was hard to right over the din of ten million rustling sequins. Wherever you are, Judi, you might like to know that the question other writers asked Ms. Faux Pas the most was: How many books did Donald Trumpet have to buy to get a walk-on in the television miniseries triumph *Princess Maisie Goes Shopping in Trumpet Tower?*

When the bell rang for dinner, Ms. Faux Pas could hardly tear herself away from the fascinating shoptalk: how to change agents, how to get even with critics, the price of a subscription to *WWWW* (the paper that covers Who's Who among Wealthy Writers), how to become a regular at one of the Tall Gals' dinner parties, how many decorating schemes one must describe to make the best-seller list, who sat next to whom at Andy Warehouse's memorial ser-

vice, and whether the $750 for tickets to the Freedom of Expression dinner was more than the average royalty on a first novel.

Up the giant staircase, Ms. Faux-Frantz ascended, when what did she see at the top of the stairs but *another* ceremonial table covered with a rug. What luck. At least the evening wasn't a total loss.

The dinner was cleverly planned as a metaphor for the writer's life: there were so many speeches that by the time the food arrived, everyone, including the ones who had forgotten, knew what it felt like to be a starving author.

Glad-Fred Steinburger made a charming welcoming speech begging people not to take home the literary-theme table decorations—the antique inkwells, Gutenberg Bibles, Shakespeare folios, first editions of Dante's *Inferno*, and the complete collection of leather-bound Book-of-the-Year Club main selections—all of which she had borrowed from the multimillion-dollar library of her husband, Billionaire Sunny Steinburger.

The finale of the glittering evening was the awarding of the door prize, Jackie Suzanna's rug, which was to go to the person who discovered the winning bookmark tucked into one of the books that were adorning the dinner tables.

It was a great moment for literacy. Glitterati who won't crack open a book unless their name is in it were rifling through the classics. Ms. Faux Pas, with uncanny prescience, reached for a slim volume on the bottom of the heap in front of her titled *The Tall Gals' How to Save the World by Marrying a Billionaire Diet and Beauty Book*. And there it was next to the title page—the prize-winning bookmark.

After posing for another picture (taken by the doorman, *naturellement*) with Glad-Fred and Norman and Broke and Sunny and Gregorian, Ms. Faux Pas rolled the lucky book inside her prize rug and headed for the all-night supermarket to get some carpet shampoo.

Since then she has been scrupulously following the Tall Gals' growth plan, which promises that by standing on your head for two hours a day you can grow an inch a year. As a fall-back position, Ms. Faux Pas is working very diligently on becoming a literary giant. *That* is a little easier to accomplish.

The next time she sees you, Ms. Faux Pas will tell you what she did when she overheard decorator Lothario Frittata tell a client that so many people were putting rugs on tables, he was thinking about doing something radical—putting rugs on the floor again.

VI

Decorating

Be My Guest

Ne quittez pas, chérie, while Ms. Faux Pas opens the reservation book to see if there is room for you at the inn next weekend. Oh dear, not then, she's redecorating. And the weekend after that Comrades Risa and Gabby Garbochef have booked. But Ms. Faux Pas would be so thrilled to have you sign her guest book the following weekend. Single or double bed, darling? How many minutes for your egg? And what is your favorite flower?

Be sure to stop by and pick up the keys—and keep the car waiting! Ms. Faux Pas's guest rooms, *comme il faut*, are six blocks from Ms. Faux Pas's living room. *A tout à l'heure*.

Life was so simple when overnight guests

stayed in the guest room in one's own apartment. Hardly anyone wanted to visit, knowing that they were sure to hear the host and hostess bickering and might have to hang their clothes in the guest room's Aspen closet, alongside the family's skis. When guests *did* come, they never overstayed their welcome.

But today, if you admit you have only a guest room for visiting firemen, your friends will take up a collection for you, poor dear. Now everyone who's anyone has a guest *apartment*—a divine satellite pied-à-terre—*several blocks away* from the family hearth. And it had better not be a one-room studio. Your private hotel must be a suite hotel—and a *toute suite* hotel (which means it must have all the right accoutrements), to boot.

No doubt the prototype for the ideal guest digs is Washington, D.C.'s Blare House—the President's guesthouse (now being redone by the chintzy House Ways and Means Committee with advice from budget deficit decorators Lothario Frittata and Clark Frampton)—where diplomatic guests can ask the staff musicians to blare "Moscow Nights." Noise control, not security, is the real reason for the heavy windowpanes being installed.

But *entre nous*, Ms. Faux Pas blames Ann Go-Getter, the high-octane socialite (and the only person with more money to burn on guests than Uncle Sam), for the escalation of the guest-room wars. The recent feature story in *Architectural Status* magazine on the Go-Getter

guest pad was the last strawberry. On top of all the other amenities one is now expected to offer guests, one must throw in one's society decorator and do the guest pad before doing the main apartment. Where will it end? Before long, a hostess will also be expected to send over her tango instructor, astrologer, personal manicurist, and a complimentary charge card from the discount drugstore to keep guests happy.

But there's no time to fret about the social rat race. The *Upwardly Mobile Travel Guide* representative is coming shortly to rate Ms. Faux Pas's guest pad and give it the white-glove test. While a low rating could knock Ms. Faux Pas out of the hospitality box altogether and make life considerably simpler, she can't resist putting on the dog and shooting for four stars. This called for upgrading the staff at her guest quarters.

Due to a misunderstanding at the employment agency where Ms. Faux Pas went to find someone who could brew a good cup of coffee in a samovar, Ms. Faux Pas, wearing her Lee Helmsleona Queen of the Palace tiara, a table favor from the recent Hospitality Industry Convention, was mistaken for a job applicant and was offered the job of Chief Housekeeper for—*quel* coincidence—Ann and Gardener Go-Getter's guest apartment.

Why not? Maybe she could pick up a few pointers on high-level hospitality.

Ms. Faux Pas's first day on the job was a

busy one. She had to supervise three seam-stresses who were making padded hangers out of antique saris to replace all the missing hangers taken by last week's guests as souve-nirs. Then Ms. Faux Pas had the staff needle-point some Go-Getter crests to put on the terrycloth robes that are so popular with house-guests they never find their way back to the laundry room. Next there were the vegetarian menus and the special arrangements for a visiting swami, a friend of a friend of Mrs. Go-Getter's.

All the furniture that had been hoisted in through the window by the power decorator when the place was furnished had to go back out through the window for the weekend because the swami believes in austerity. Ms. Faux Pas couldn't help noticing, however, that the swami, like most guests, didn't leave empty-handed. He was swathed in one of the hostess's exquisitely embroidered sheets, and in his knapsack he had stuffed a handsomely framed photo of the long-stemmed Mrs. Go-Getter in her bathing suit. Apparently the picture is so popular with guests that Mrs. G. keeps a whole stack of them—each in its own antique frame—in the linen closet. However, the Go-Getters' generos-ity doesn't extend to the antique silver flatware, the miniature bronze collection, or the precious Jasper Pollock painting, all of which have been rigged to beep when anyone tries to smuggle them out. Reproductions are available on re-quest from the housekeeper.

Ms. Faux Pas's last responsibility before she left (there were problems, as you'll see) was looking after the reviewer from the *Upwardly Mobile Travel Guide*. Needless to say, she had mixed emotions about helping him have a nice day at a guest apartment that was not her own. Somehow, she forgot to pick up all the fallen flower petals that had looked so *je ne sais quoi* in the *Architectural Status* photos, but which do not pass the white-glove test.

She also forgot to take the swami's leftover veggieburgers out of the guest bedroom refrig-erator; forgot to take the angora bed jacket out of the freezer; forgot to stand up the needle-point pillow that reads, You *Are* Leaving on Sunday, Aren't You?; forgot to turn the forks over—prongs down—when she set the table; forgot to put the guest's brass nameplate in the slot in the bedroom door; forgot to leave the *Book of Sayings from Famous Guestbooks*, pub-lished by Mrs. Go-Getter's small press, under the reviewer's pillow; forgot to change the blown bulbs in the makeup mirror. She also left two wire hangers in the closet.

When the next edition of the *Upwardly Mo-bile Travel Guide* came out, Ms. Faux Pas was pleased to see that her own guest pad had two more stars than the Go-Getters'.

Ms. Faux Pas admits that she is paying for her little charade with a constantly booked guest apartment. Meanwhile, the grateful Mrs. Go-Getter—who has saved a bundle on terry-cloth robe replacement expenses now that she has only a 75 percent occupancy rate—recently sent Ms. Faux Pas a *très* apropos thank-you gift. It's a needlepoint pillow that reads, You Never Know How Many Friends You Have Until You Have a Guest Apartment. *A bientôt.*

The next time she sees you, Ms. Faux Pas will tell you how embarrassing it was to stand on the cloth-coat checkroom line at the ballet when tout le monde *was on the fur-coat line.*

The "Next Color" Will Be ...

While most of the executives Ms. Faux Pas meets at the watercooler are worrying about the color of their parachutes, Ms. Faux Pas is worrying about the color of her bathing suit. Lest you assume she is headed for *la plage*, Ms. Faux Pas hastens to explain that she has just been invited to join a Think Tank, and she is looking for something appropriate to wear to her first session—in addition to her thinking cap.

Frankly, Ms. Faux Pas is accustomed to doing her thinking *toute seule*, and *au naturel*, in the hot tub. But now that she is going to be doing her thinking among others, she thought that dressing for success in this instance called for a tank suit.

Perhaps Ms. Faux Pas should explain right here that her Think Tank has a narrower focus than that of giants like SRI or the Rand Corporation. Ms. Faux Pas will definitely not be called upon to think about the number of grandfather clocks that can be sold to yuppies, or ponder worst-case scenarios in the event of World War IV.

Ms. Faux Pas's tank—the Think Pink Tank—has only one mission: to predict the colors people-like-us will want on their wallpaper three years hence.

If you promise not to splash it about, Ms. Faux Pas will confess that Chauncey the paperhanger has been patiently sitting on his ladder in the middle of Ms. Faux Pas's drawing room for the past month, waiting for her to make up her mind about what color wallpaper she wants—this year.

Actually, she did make up her mind, but certain people are trying to get her to change it. Ms. Faux Pas had a yen to paper her drawing room in Nouvelle Bellini—the color of the peach-juice-and-champagne Bellini cocktail, the drink of the year. Bellini Peach is also the color of the wallpaper at every nouvelle cuisine bistro worth its *sel*. But Ms. Faux Pas's decorator, Billy Armoire, has decreed that Bellini Peach is passé.

Not only is peach passé, but all colors named for foods are passé, says Brother Armoire (as Billy is called by people whose drawing rooms are paid for in full). This eliminates Apricot, Rhubarb, Melon, Raspberry, and, Ms. Faux Pas gives thanks, Avocado. Obviously, there's a lot of thinking about color to be done at the tank if the wallpaper industry is going to have any colors left to sell.

You are probably wondering why Ms. Faux Pas doesn't just ask Billy Armoire point-blank what the next color will be. He knows, of course, and is aching to tell, but can't divulge it until his latest decorating opus is published in *Architectural Status*. The magazine's editor, Page Turner, worries so much about being scooped that not even Billy Armoire's *clients* are allowed to see the new color scheme until it's published. Billy has supplied them with chintz blindfolds.

But Ms. Faux Pas is not going to hang around the corner newsstand in a wet bathing suit waiting for the *Architectural Status* shipment to come in—she is going to unearth the next color on her own. Color forecasting, she suspects, is no harder to master than bargello—a hobby of Ms. Faux Pas's that has yielded, so far, a dozen passé peach and avocado scatter pillows.

For her first foray into color prediction, Ms. Faux Pas designed a simple consumer experiment. She placed a jar of assorted colored crayons on every table at Biff McMorton's—the bistro where people-like-us lunch with their decorators while tormenting them with client indecision—and she waited behind the flower arrangement to see which colors would disappear fastest.

Chauncey the paperhanger, who has more than a passing interest in Ms. Faux Pas's results, was betting on purple—the color of the bridesmaids' dresses at Caroline O'Kennedy's wedding (a color couldn't get better media exposure if it paid for it); purple is also the new "in" color in designer vegetables—peas, peppers, potatoes, broccoli, and okra—according to the Gray Lady, the *New York Times on My Hands*. And besides, pointed out Chauncey, who has been watching a lot of TV talk shows up there on the ladder, *The Color Aubergine* certainly made a lot of money for Hollywood. (As any press agent pushing a color knows, no hue can make it big until it stars in a major motion picture.)

But Ms. Faux Pas is not convinced. If purple is so important, why didn't Judi Frantz, that legendary authority on the color tastes of people-like-us, give lavender eyes to Moxie Amberville, the heroine of Miss Frantz's new best-seller, *I'll Take a Manhattan?* Moxie's eyes are not violet, blue, gray, hazel, or amber. They are green. And the mother-of-the-bride gown worn recently by Jackie O'No-Photographs was not lavender, but celadon green. And Ms. Faux Pas just realized what happens to purple vegetables when they are cooked—they turn green. Before Ms. Faux Pas had even counted the missing crayons, it was obvious. Green is the Next Color.

Ms. Faux Pas is in a blue funk at the thought. This will take some getting used to. Green—the most popular color for American cars in 1928; the color on instant-coffee labels that signifies decaffeination; the color of Ms. Faux Pas's plastic surgeon's scrub suit; the color that Kandinsky called bourgeois; and the color of the algae in the Think Tank.

Meanwhile, the evidence is in at Biff Mc-Morton's bistro—all the green crayons disappeared on the first night. The word is spreading like kudzu. All the copper roofs in the city seem to have turned peacock green overnight; green subway cars are rolling underground; Paul Blue-Eyes's *The Color of Cash* has arrived on the silver screen. What's more, Billy Armoire, now wearing green contact lenses, has given his clients permission to take off their chintz blindfolds. Leaping lizards! Though they were expecting Bellini Peach, they love the idea that they're the first on their block with the Next Color. And it doesn't hurt that their friends are all green with envy.

Meanwhile, in verdant southern California, fickle Page Turner is sending out a memo to all her pet designers that she will not publish any more green rooms. And GE is bringing back avocado appliances—but will probably call them Spruce since the Next Names for colors are all very verdant.

But the grass is not greener in Ms. Faux Pas's drawing room. Even though Ms. Faux Pas knows she has to go green, Chauncey,

unfortunately, is still stuck on the ladder because Ms. Faux Pas cannot decide which *shade*
of green she wants. And then—of course—it
dawns on her. She'll paper the room in Authen-
tic Treasury Green, the color on the back of
newly printed five-hundred-dollar bills. Instead
of the passé peach of Nouvelle Bellini, Ms.
Faux Pas's drawing room will be the *au
courant, au currency* green of Nouveau Riche.
   And that's really the Next Color.

*The next time she sees you, Ms. Faux Pas will tell
you how she reacted when Page Turner acciden-
tally (?) spilled her Bellini on Ms. Faux Pas's
spruce green divan while reaching for a purple
crudité.*

VII

Politics

Pillow Talk

Q uel summer, *mes amis.* Ms. Faux Pas was so busy turning last season's pouf dress into a skinny mini, she hardly had time to finish the talking pillow she's been needlepointing for Harry Hartthrob. You remember Harry, don't you? He's the Democratic unhopeful who dared the fourth estate to trail him so they could see how dull his private life was, and who, when it was discovered his private life wasn't *that* dull, refused to answer the A (for adultery) question: "Did you ever commit A?"

Ms. Faux Pas's friends insist it's a little late for campaign presents to Harry, but on the outside chance that he's planning to change his name yet again in an attempt to take his water bed into the Off-White House, Ms. Faux Pas wants to have a little pillow talk with him.

The Harry Hartthrob affair might have had a different ending if Harry had indulged in pillow talk of a different kind. But how could Harry learn the ropes when he was having his fund-raising affairs in trendy peach-colored restaurants with yuppies clad in Safe Sex T-shirts instead of in Establishment living rooms, where he would have been exposed to the real rules of etiquette—the ones the glitterati display on their scatter pillows lest anyone forget.

For example, Lana Riviera, widow of the eye-shadow king, has a pillow embroidered with her credo: "You can never own too big a yacht or wear your hair too long or your skirts too short." Billionaire Ronny Pearldiver, the current eye-shadow king, and his gossip-reporter wife, Eye-Claudia, have a pillow that proclaims: "No matter how much eye makeup you wear or how small the type on the eye chart, you can always read the letters LBO" (for Leveraged Buy-Out, *chéries*).

Nancy Reaganomics has a much-copied pillow that reads, "Just Say No"—which is good advice these days but probably hard for a Democrat to take. And Bubbly Waters, the TV interviewer who got an exclusive face-to-face with Karolina Rice (Harry Hartthrob's pillow talkee), has a pillow reading, "Ask tough questions, but never answer them."

But every glitterati house worth its vermeil saltcellars has one pillow needlepointed with the commandment that could have saved Harry's campaign. It reads, "A is Okay, but Never on Weekends." (Harry will soon have such a pillow, needlepointed by Ms. Faux Pas. Better late than never.)

If Harry Hartthrob had brought Karolina Rice over to his place for a little dictation on a Tuesday lunch hour, no one would have given it a second thought. If she stayed late, he could have said they were watching the nightly news together. A is still Okay, but there's a time and a place for everything.

As anyone who reads *Peephole* magazine knows, the unfortunate Harry chose to do his controversial partying on weekends. The only people who party on weekends from September to June are the regularati—the people who read about the glitterati in the Sunday papers.

But to the glitterati themselves, weekends are sacred. They are meant to be spent with the family, at the country home. Think about it. Have you ever noticed a big social event or charity ball taking place on a weekend? Only in July or August are glitterati parties held on weekends—and then only at the summer resorts frequented by them and their families.

When Bubbly Waters celebrated the first anniversary of her third marriage with a bash for a thousand people recently, it wasn't on a weekend—none of her buddies would have been in town. When Kate Grahamcracker, publisher of the *Washington Post-Dispatch*, gathered several hundred friends for her birthday this year, she did it on a Tuesday. And last spring's most spectacular glitterati party, Malcolm Fourbits's fly-by-night anniversary party for *F*, his funny money magazine, took place on a Thursday on Mr. Fourbits's helicopter landing pad in New Jersey.

Another reason that A is Okay, but Never on Weekends, is that the press is too busy during the week covering parties such as Malcolm Fourbits's to stake out a candidate's house. No one would have noticed Karolina Rice going into Harry Hartthrob's home on a weeknight.

After Harry Hartthrob refused to answer the A question, there was a lot of speculation on *Nightlife*, the sanctimonious late-night news show, that mores had changed in the last twenty years. It was recalled that at least one former president (and possibly thirty-two) allegedly got away with A repeatedly but was never subjected to the A question.

Ms. Faux Pas believes this particular former president was never asked the A question because he did his pillow talking during the week on his lunch hour. On weekends, like a good glitterati, he watched the family play touch football.

Of course, if we're being totally frank and honest, we must mention that the touch-football-on-weekends tradition is not the only reason glitterati hold parties during the week. This media-conscious crowd knows that a party has a better chance of making *Timely* or *Peephole* if it's held early in the week. Now, we

know Harry Hartthrob doesn't want his private parties in *Peephole*—but that's all the more reason to have them during the week, preferably on the same night Malcolm Fourbits is having a wingding. What reporter wants to stand around watching the driveway at Harry Hartthrob's when he could be on the tarmac at Mr. Fourbits's watching Liz Customtailor and 1,199 other glitterati deplane for a barbecue? If Harry Hartthrob had planned his pillow talk by the social calendar and *Peephole* magazine's deadlines, he could have committed A right there on his driveway—by klieg light!—and Karolina Rice would never have made the cover of *Peephole* or become a household word.

That's the way it is, as Uncle Walter used to say. And if Harry Hartthrob or anyone else refuses to live by the rules of the glitterati, he'll have to live by the pillow slogan of the Republicans and "Just Say No." *N'est-ce pas?*

The next time she sees you, Ms. Faux Pas will thank Fawn Hallmark for that nice bag of shredded pillow stuffing.

Takeovers and
Make-Overs

Après *vous* on the down escalator, *chérie*. Ever since the Mona Lisa Museum in Paris announced it was expanding down under, it seems as if all the parties Ms. Faux Pas is invited to are underground affairs. First there was the hard-hat party launching La Place des Puces, a posh underground flea market in Manhattan.

Then there was the subway bash in honor of the Guardian Anglers. And, most recently, Ms. Faux Pas was invited to the opening in our nation's capital of a new underground museum for aboveground art.

Quel coincidence. Ms. Faux Pas was going to be in Washington that week for a convention of the Emily Postscript Society, the organization of etiquette writers. This is the group whose motto is, "If we can be courteous to fellow etiquette advisers, we can be courteous to anyone." Ms. Faux Pas was to be a speaker. Her topic: "How Polite Is Too Polite? Or, Why No One Wants to Tell Judge Mork What Is Keeping Him from Being Confirmed."

The night before her speech, Ms. Faux Pas dropped in on the opening of the underground museum. *Mon Dieu*, it was a strange crowd. Even the waiters wore trench coats and carried walkie-talkies, the latest style in Washington, where the outfit is meant to confuse Russian diplomats, who suspect that every American they encounter is in the BIA—the Bungled Intelligence Agency.

One charming man in a trench coat with walkie-talkie engaged Ms. Faux Pas in earnest conversation, hinting that the government had a unique personnel problem that she might be able to solve. He seemed well aware of Ms. Faux Pas's spectacular etiquette coups.

One of her major successes was the use of good manners to deter Ashley Ableman, the Columbus University Business School lecturer and Wall Street takeover specialist, from taking over Ms. Faux Pas's Bread-and-Butter Note Company. When Mr. Ableman sent his greenmail letter, Ms. Faux Pas didn't panic. She diplomatically wired him a gracious reply via Telexit, declining his generous tender offer and suggesting that the *real* growth potential was to be found in *electronic* bread-and-butter notes.

As *tout le monde* knows by now, that little tip resulted in Mr. Ableman's raiding Telexit instead. Ms. Faux Pas is politely awaiting her finder's fee.

But perhaps Ms. Faux Pas's most brilliant coup was her most recent one: the White House chief of protocol turned to Ms. Faux Pas as a last resort in an effort to get President Reaganomics to stop saying "Over my dead body" every time someone suggested he balance his Off-White House budget. Her solution? She just called billionaire Donald Trumpet and tipped him off that the President was thinking of getting a low-cost long-distance service to cut down on Off-White House phone bills for calls to senators opposed to Judge Mork, which could cause AT&T to tumble, which could affect the market seriously.

The rest is history. As everyone knows, Mr. Trumpet dumped his whole stock portfolio, thereby precipitating the stock market adjustment of October 19—which got the President to start taking his unbalanced budget seriously and stop saying "Over my dead body."

If Ms. Faux Pas couldn't solve the government's etiquette problem, who could? The man in the trench coat slipped Ms. Faux Pas a note: "Meet me at the bottom of the down escalator at 7:23. Come alone. Have a nice day."

Before she had time to wonder what the great problem could be, it was time to keep her appointment. The charming young man led her down a corridor, through a hidden door, and—voilà!—she was suddenly in the Awkward Situation Room in the subbasement of the BIA. Ms. Faux Pas's task? At the President's request, she was to help Judge Mork shed his undeserved (at least, in the President's opinion) Frankenstein image, which was keeping him from being confirmed for a seat on the Court of Last Resort. This was a tough one, since the judge had no inkling of why he was having no influence over anyone in the court of public opinion.

Ms. Faux Pas was certain *she* knew the reason he was having trouble—but ever since Tiny Tim got married on *The Tonight Show*, it's been considered bad manners to stereotype people by hairstyle. The buzz phrase for "see your barber" is now *groom for success*. But as every etiquette adviser knows, you can't tell someone point-blank that he needs a make-over. It's kinder to get the subject to identify the problem himself. So Ms. Faux Pas pulled out her trusty image counselor's guide and opened up to the chapter called How Not to Make Friends and Influence People, featuring bearded celebrities who could never sell a used car to a senator: Bluebeard, Mephistopheles, Rasputin, and Blackbeard.

Ms. Faux Pas asked Judge Mork to tell her what all these men had in common that would make them unsuited to influence the U.S. Senate parking lot. "They are all famous in the annals of law," he said, missing the point altogether, as he often does. This, Ms. Faux Pas realized, was going to be a hard one. Then the judge went on to discuss their cases. As for Bluebeard, who was mean to his wives, the judge said that while he didn't agree with Bluebeard's actions *personally*, if the founding fathers had wanted wives to be equals, they would have given women the vote; concerning the allegedly raw deal the Devil gave Faust, "It was a legal contract," the judge said, "freely arrived at and not subject to government interference"; as for Rasputin, the social walker of the Czarina, like any lobbyist he "was entitled to seek access to power and free use of his hypnotic powers"; and in the case of Blackbeard, the pirate, "He should not be restrained from aggressively maximizing his profits in the maritime market." The judge saw no resemblance between himself and these men.

Taking the bull by the goatee, Ms. Faux Pas came right to the point and said that beards, although they can impart a professorial look, on occasion—especially this occasion—could give one a sinister look, interfering with the perception of one's better qualities. Thus, she suggested a clean shave. The judge, taken aback, said that would be an invasion of his right to privacy, if he had one, which he didn't believe he had. But he said he'd keep an open mind, if he had one, which most people aren't sure he has. After thinking it over, the conservative judge for once refused to split hairs, with the result that, as everyone knows by now, he lost the confirmation vote.

For Ms. Faux Pas, it wasn't a total loss. The BIA didn't cancel her consulting contract. In fact, the moles there gave her a walkie-talkie and a trench coat and recommended her to the Russian embassy as an image consultant for the Garbochefs, on the premise that people who dress like capitalists are more likely to think like capitalists. In addition, the etiquette society awarded Ms. Faux Pas its prestigious Truth in Counseling Award. *Formidable!*

The next time she sees you, Ms. Faux Pas will explain why Premier Garbochef postponed the summit with President Reaganomics. Entre nous, the new suits the premier had ordered from a London haberdasher (at Ms. Faux Pas's urging) weren't ready.

Kiss and Tell

Défense de stationner in front of the Secretive Service car. But don't cry for Ms. Faux Pas because she's under house surveillance. The handsome men with the walkie-talkies sitting on her doorstep make her feel so safe and secure. They've been trailing her and tapping her phone ever since Ms. Faux Pas contacted *journaliste* Kitty Tell-it-all in order to get a load off her chest of drawers—actually a *car*load of dirty laundry lists from a certain past President who kissed Ms. Faux Pas, but she never told about it. Until now.

Liz Smithereens, the breathless gossip columnist of the *Daily Who's News*, has encouraged Ms. Faux Pas to come clean. Liz says keeping mum is as old hat as Studio 53; today you are nobody unless you expose the ring around your collar to *Peephole* magazine.

Of course, Liz has a vested interest in getting people with a past like Ms. Faux Pas's to fess up. If folks with X-rated memories didn't confess now and then, Liz Smithereens would be spending her evenings covering fires in Hoboken instead of such hot glitterati events as Donald Trumpet's book burning and Malcolm Fourbits's barbecues.

Some people, who remember bumping into Ms. Faux Pas at suspicious times and places in Washington way back *when*, have always suspected that Ms. Faux Pas was involved in some Off-White House hanky-panky, but Ms. Faux Pas always whitewashed the suspicion. She believed that taking the President's dirty laundry out of the hamper was dangerous to national security. But now that hardly anyone is alive to dispute her version of history, Ms. Faux Pas feels ready to go public.

Perhaps you're surprised that Ms. Faux Pas is a woman who wasn't bored yesterday. Didn't you think she was the type to have the password to the dirty-laundry room at the Off-White House?

Actually it all started quite innocently many years ago, during what came to be known as the Cuban Button Crisis on the Day of Pigskin. Ms. Faux Pas, at that time an aspiring etiquette adviser, was being interviewed for a job as a good-manners intern in the protocol office of the Off-White House, when, by a quirk of fate, she was catapulted into history. While she was taking a handwriting test, an urgent call came from the Oval Office. The President had popped a button on his shirt while playing touch football with his brothers, and the presidential valet (the First Button Sewer) was out picking up a new pigskin from the Redskins. The First Lady (who, if she knew how to sew buttons, had never volunteered for the job) was off in the Mediterranean with her sister on some millionaire's yacht.

Alas, the President, who undoubtedly had other shirts in his chifforobe, couldn't change, because the shirt with the missing button had been a gift from a group of Cuban exiles who were expected at any moment for a photo opportunity. Certainly none of the President's men wanted to have to affront the Cubans by admitting that the President didn't have all his buttons. It was bad enough he was smoking contraband cigars from Havana.

The office of protocol was in an uproar. None of the properly finished finishing-school ladies who had been hired for their ability to write proper thank-you notes knew how to sew buttons. The best they could do was embroider initials on handkerchiefs that they gave to their beaux as mementos. And none of the Secretive Service men would admit to being able even to thread a needle, for fear of what J. Edgar Behoover would call them.

But the handy Ms. Faux Pas had nothing to

lose. She couldn't help overhearing the hub-bub, and patriotically volunteered for button duty, whipping out her trusty sewing kit, which she always carried in her purse. It was a gift from her great-aunt Martha, who had told her that a stitch in time got Betsy Ross ahead in government. All that was needed was security clearance from J. Edgar himself, and a pair of dark glasses so the other protocol interns wouldn't be able to tattle to gossip columnists about whom the President had taken his shirt off for.

Ms. Faux Pas was ushered into the President's dressing room by a phalanx of burly Secretive Service operatives. From behind a dressing screen the bare-chested President handed his shirt to an aide, who handed it to Ms. Faux Pas, who never before had had such an illustrious audience watch her sew a simple button. After the President was fully dressed again, he commended Ms. Faux Pas profusely, giving her an innocent peck on the cheek.

As she turned to leave, the President asked if Ms. Faux Pas knew a good hand laundry for his shirts, which often had lipstick on them because he had to kiss so many people when he gave out Presidential Commendations. Ms. Faux Pas suggested a little-known laundry favored by fussy men who dabbled in concrete. Actually, she had earned pin money from the laundry when she was working her way through college by sewing up the holes in clients' bul-letproof vests. She told the President that if Mr. Behoover would give her clearance, she would be happy to personally pick up and deliver a box of shirts every week. The President asked her if he could also include his embroidered hankies, which he didn't feel his wife had to see when she sorted the laundry. And that's how Ms. Faux Pas got the key to the dirty-laundry room at the Off-White House.

Now Ms. Faux Pas hears that some Other Woman is telling *Peephole* that *she* had the key to the Off-White House dirty-laundry room. The Other Woman must have been stuck with the pajamas. Ms. Faux Pas assures you there was only one needle—hers—involved in the Cu-ban Button Crisis. She doesn't have it any-more—the President asked her if he could stick it in the Fidelity Castro voodoo doll given him by the BIA (the Bungled Intelligence Agency). But Ms. Faux Pas kept the sewing kit and recently donated it, along with all her extra buttons, to the Kitty Tell-it-all Collection of Bankable Memorabilia at the New York Notorious Li-brary.

The only other thing necessary to put Ms. Faux Pas's mind at ease is her friends' forgiveness for her long silence about this secret part of her life. Only now can she confess her suspicions that the laundry was delivering contraband Havana cigars to the Off-White House in the boxes that contained the President's hankies. In fact, Ms. Faux Pas will be in Washington next week, giving the unembroidered truth under oath about the

Off-White House hanky-panky. If anyone
doubts Ms. Faux Pas's version of events, she
can describe details of the decor of the
President's private dressing room that have
never been disclosed before and could only be
known by someone who was there: there was a
Marilyn Monrose calendar on the inside of his
closet door. *Vraiment!*

ACKNOWLEDGMENTS

Ms. Faux Pas's Nouvelle Manners column was born out of desperation after Clay Felker missed his deadline for a last-page essay in AVENUE. Once again he can take the blame for encouraging this writer's career. The inspiration for the first piece (thanks especially to Mario Buatta and Sue Newhouse) was the seventy-fifth anniversary party for the New York Public Library, where the Glit-Lit crowd dined on salad with their fingers. Since then, the author has never taken the glitterati seriously.

While Ms. Faux Pas insists she is the power behind many of *them*, behind Ms. Faux Pas herself is a loyal troupe of colleagues who have pretended to find her amusing, tried to fix her syntax, her French, and her malapropisms to no avail, and encouraged her (probably mistakenly) in innumerable ways.

Her mentor has been Alan Halpern, who always laughs at Ms. Faux Pas's jokes—and has been known to improve them.

Barbara Lish originally selected Michael Witte—the perfect choice—to illustrate Ms. Faux Pas, and he has brought another dimension to the character.

It's an understatement to say that Andrew Wilkes made this book happen. Carlo Barile lavished his attention on the book's design. Anne Nolan was a proficient copy editor in English *and* French. In addition, a host of former and present colleagues at AVENUE, especially Mindy Ball, William Grimes, Clare Herrmann, John Nash, Susan Roy, Steven Friedlander, and Jennifer Lonoff, all helped Ms. Faux Pas find her voice, not to mention her galleys.

Arthur Abelman, Carol Addessi, Walter Bernard, Henry Burr, Rose Feldman, Stanley Feldman, Michael Fragnito, Daniel Kron, Jane Marder, Jerry Marder, Jonathan Marder, Betsy Nolan, Gloria Plaut, Don Reick, Stanley Rothenberg, Howard Rubenstein, Judy Tabak, and Susan Zelouf all offered their expertise and advice. Some of it was taken.

Merci beaucoup to them all!

—J. K.

ABOUT THE AUTHOR

Joan Kron is the editor in chief of AVENUE. Before that, she was an
irreverent staff writer and editor for several publications, including
the *Wall Street Journal,* the *New York Times, New York,* and *Philadelphia.*
This is her third book. She is the coauthor of *High-Tech: The Industrial
Style and Source Book for the Home* (Potter, 1978) and the author of
Home-Psych: The Social Psychology of Home and Decoration
(Potter, 1983).
She is also the founder of Parvenu Press.

INDEX

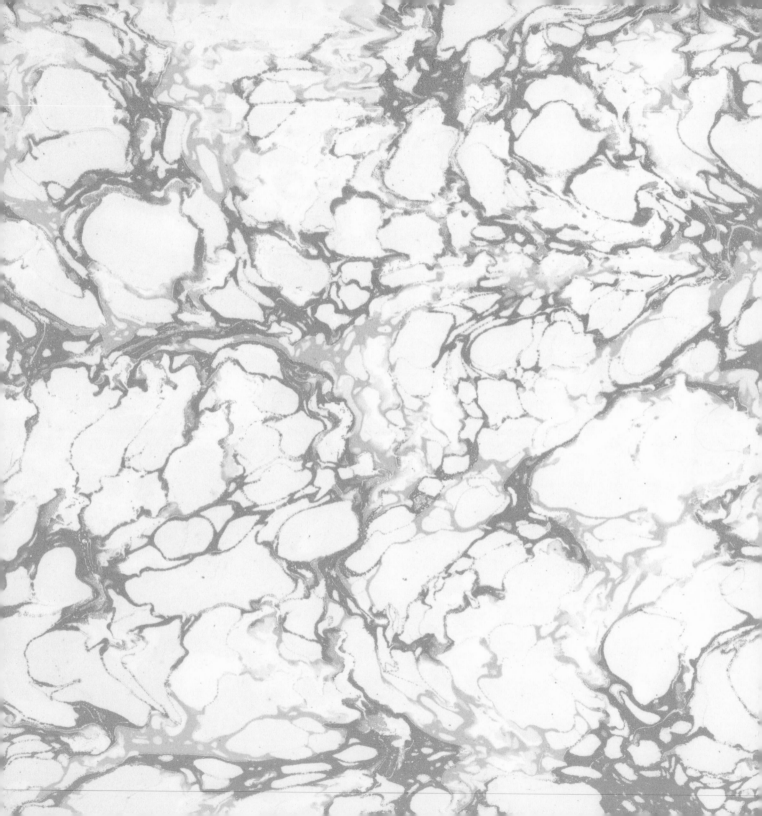